Good Questions for Math Teaching

Why Ask Them and What to Ask, K–6

Peter Sullivan
Pat Lilburn

Math Solutions Publications
Sausalito, CA

Math Solutions Publications
150 Gate 5 Road
Sausalito, CA 94965
www.mathsolutions.com

First published in Australia as *Open-Ended Maths Activities: Using Good Questions to Enhance Learning* by Peter Sullivan and Pat Lilburn (ISBN 0-19-554099-9) by Oxford University Press, Australia, © 1997 Peter Sullivan, Pat Lilburn.

First U.S. printing 2002 by Math Solutions Publications. Adapted by permission of Oxford University Press. Copyright © Oxford University Press.

Library of Congress Cataloging-in-Publication Data
Sullivan, Peter, 1948–
    [Open-ended maths activities]
    Good questions for math teaching : why ask them and what to ask, K–6 /
Peter Sullivan, Pat Lilburn.
            p. cm.
Originally published: Open-ended maths activities. Australia : Oxford University
    Press, c1997.
        ISBN 0-941355-51-9 (acid-free paper)
    1. Mathematics—Study and teaching (Elementary) 2. Questioning. I. Lilburn, Pat.
    II. Title.
        QA135.6 .S85 2002
            372.7'044—dc21

                                                                    2002009229

ISBN-13: 978-0-941355-51-3
ISBN-10: 0-941355-51-9

Editor: Toby Gordon
Production: Melissa L. Inglis
Cover design: Catherine Hawkes/Cat and Mouse
Interior design: Joni Doherty Design
Composition: Tom Allen

Printed in the United States of America on acid-free paper
11 10 09 08   ML   10

SFI CERTIFIED SOURCING
FIBER USED IN THIS PRODUCT LINE MEETS THE SOURCING REQUIREMENTS OF THE SFI PROGRAM
WWW.SFIPROGRAM.ORG

A Message from Marilyn Burns

We at Math Solutions Professional Development believe that teaching math well calls for increasing our understanding of the math we teach, seeking deeper insights into how children learn mathematics, and refining our lessons to best promote students' learning.

Math Solutions Publications shares classroom-tested lessons and teaching expertise from our faculty of Math Solutions Inservice instructors as well as from other respected math educators. Our publications are part of the nationwide effort we've made since 1984 that now includes

- more than five hundred face-to-face inservice programs each year for teachers and administrators in districts across the country;
- annually publishing professional development books, now totaling more than seventy titles and spanning the teaching of all math topics in kindergarten through grade 8;
- four series of videos for teachers, plus a video for parents, that show math lessons taught in actual classrooms;
- on-site visits to schools to help refine teaching strategies and assess student learning; and
- free online support, including grade-level lessons, book reviews, inservice information, and district feedback, all in our *Math Solutions Online Newsletter.*

For information about all of the products and services we have available, please visit our website at *www.mathsolutions.com.* You can also contact us to discuss math professional development needs by calling (800) 868-9092 or by sending an email to *info@mathsolutions.com.*

We're always eager for your feedback and interested in learning about your particular needs. We look forward to hearing from you.

Math Solutions®

Contents

Acknowledgments

The idea of open-ended or good questions developed over several years during ongoing discussions between Peter Sullivan and David Clarke.

Peter and David conducted a number of research studies and classroom trials of open-ended questions. Many of David's initial ideas are used in various places throughout this book. His creativity, energy, and interest in exploring good questions contributed significantly to the idea of using open-ended activities in the teaching of mathematics, and for this we thank him.

The idea went through a number of phases before it reached its final form. Pam Rawson's contribution to the early planning stages, which ultimately led to the development of this resource, is greatly appreciated.

Finally, we thank Sheryl and Mike without whose continued support there would be no book.

PETER SULLIVAN
PAT LILBURN

PART **O**NE

The Importance of Questioning

During the course of a normal school day teachers ask many questions. In fact, something like 60 percent of the things said by teachers are questions and most of these are not planned.

One way of categorizing questions is to describe them as either *open* or *closed*. Closed questions are those that simply require an answer or a response to be given from memory, such as a description of a situation or object or the reproduction of a skill. Open questions are those that require a student to think more deeply and to give a response that involves more than recalling a fact or reproducing a skill.

Teachers are usually skilled at asking open questions in content areas such as language arts or social studies. For example, teachers often ask children to interpret situations or justify opinions. However, in mathematics lessons closed questions are much more common.

Questions that encourage students to do more than recall known facts have the potential to stimulate thinking and reasoning. To emphasize problem solving, application, and the development of a variety of thinking skills it is vital that we pay more attention to improving our questioning in mathematics lessons. Teachers should use questions that develop their students' higher levels of thinking.

Good Questions for Math Teaching looks in more detail at a particular type of open question that we call a "good" question. Our goals of education are for our students to think, to learn, to analyze, to criticize, and to be able to solve unfamiliar problems, and it follows that good questions should be part of the instructional repertoire of all teachers of mathematics.

In this book we describe the features of good questions, show how to create good questions, give some practical ideas for using them in your classroom, and provide many good questions that you can use in your mathematics program.

1 What Are Good Questions?

Let us have a closer look at what makes a good question. There are three main features of good questions.

- They require more than remembering a fact or reproducing a skill.
- Students can learn by answering the questions, and the teacher learns about each student from the attempt.
- There may be several acceptable answers.

This section explains these features in more detail.

More Than Remembering

A particular grade 6 student, Jane, had just finished a unit on measurement where she had been asked to calculate area and perimeter from diagrams of rectangles with the dimensions marked. She was able to complete these correctly, and the teacher assumed from this that Jane understood the concepts of area and perimeter. However, when she was asked the following good question she claimed that she could not do it because there was not enough information given. *I want to make a garden in the shape of a rectangle. I have 30 meters of fence for my garden. What might be the area of the garden?*

To find an answer to this Jane needed to think about the constraints that a perimeter of 30 meters places on the lengths of the sides of the rectangle, as well as thinking about the area. She needed to use higher order reasoning skills since she had to consider the relationship of area and perimeter to find possible whole number answers that could range from 14 x 1 (14m^2) to 7 x 8 (56m^2). This certainly required her to do more than remember a fact or reproduce a skill. It required comprehension of the task, application of the concepts and appropriate skills, and analysis and some synthesis of the two major concepts involved.

Through further probing, this question allowed the teacher to see that Jane had little appreciation of perimeter as the distance around a region, and no concept of area as covering. She had learned to answer routine exercises without fully understanding the concepts.

Another example of closed questions commonly found in textbooks is from the topic of averages. A typical question looks something like *What is the average of 6, 7, 5, 8, and 4?* This mainly requires students to recall a technique. That is, add the numbers and divide by how many there are—in this case five. However, if this question was rephrased in the form of a good question it would look something like *The average of five numbers is 6. What might the numbers be?* or *After five games, the goalie had averaged blocking six goals per game. What might be the number of goals he blocked in each game?*

These questions require a different level of thinking and a different type of understanding of the topic of averages to be able to give an answer. Students need to comprehend and analyze the task. They must have a clear idea of the concept of average and either use the principle that the scores are evenly placed about the average or that the total of the scores is 30 (that is, 5 x 6) as the basis of their response. It most definitely requires more than remembering.

Students Learn By Answering the Question and Teachers Learn from the Students' Attempts

Good questions are particularly suitable for this because they have the potential to make children more aware of what they do know and what they do not know. That is, students can become aware of where their understanding is incomplete. The earlier question about area and perimeter showed that by thinking about area and perimeter together the student is made aware of the fact that the area can change even though the perimeter is fixed. The very act of trying to complete the question can help children gain a better understanding of the concepts involved. The manner in which some children went about answering the following question illustrates this point.

> John and Maria each measured the length of the basketball court. John said that it was 25 yardsticks long, and Maria said that it was 24 $\frac{1}{2}$ yardsticks long. How could this happen?

Some fifth- and sixth-grade students were asked to discuss this question in groups. They suggested a variety of plausible explanations and were then asked to suggest what they need to think about when measuring length. Their list included the need to:

- agree on levels of accuracy
- agree on where to start and finish, and the importance of starting at the zero on the yardstick
- avoid overlap at the ends of the yardsticks
- avoid spaces between the yardsticks
- measure the shortest distance in a straight line.

By answering the question the students established for themselves these essential aspects of measurement, and thus learned by doing the task.

As we have discussed, the way students respond to good questions can also show the teacher if they understand the concept and can give a clear indication of where further work is needed. If Jane's teacher had not presented her with the good question she would have thought Jane totally understood the concepts of area and perimeter. In the above example, the teacher could see that the children did understand how to use an instrument to measure accurately. Thus we can see that good questions are useful as assessment tools, too.

Several Acceptable Answers

Many of the questions teachers ask, especially during mathematics lessons, have only one correct answer. Such questions are perfectly acceptable, but there are many other questions that have more than one possible answer and teachers should make a point of asking these, too. Each of the good questions that we have already looked at has several possible answers. Because of this, these questions foster higher level thinking because they encourage students to develop their problem-solving expertise at the same time as they are acquiring mathematical skills.

There are different levels of sophistication at which individual students might respond. It is characteristic of such good questions that each student can make a valid response that reflects the extent of their understanding. Since correct answers can be given at a number of levels, such tasks are particularly appropriate for mixed ability classes. Students who respond quickly at a superficial level can be asked to look for alternative or more general solutions. Other students will recognize these alternatives and search for a general solution.

If we think back to the earlier question on the area of the garden, there is a range of acceptable whole number answers (14 x 1, 13 x 2, 12 x 3 . . . 8 x 7). Students could be asked to find the largest or smallest garden possible. They could be asked to describe all possible rectangles. Other students will be interested in exploring answers other than those that involve only whole numbers, for example, 12.5m x 2.5m. It is the openness of the task that provides this richness. The existence of several acceptable answers stimulates the higher level thinking and the problem solving.

In this section, we have looked more closely at the three features that categorize good questions. We have seen that the quality of learning is related both to the tasks given to students and to the quality of questions the teacher asks. Students can learn mathematics better if they work on questions or tasks that require more than recall of information, and from which they can learn by the act of answering the question, and that allow for a range of possible answers.

Good questions possess these features and therefore should be regarded as an important teaching tool for teachers to develop. The next section shows two ways to construct your own good questions.

How to Create Good Questions

Good questions can be used as the basis for an entire lesson either as a lesson that stands alone or as part of a unit of work. It is possible to make up your own good questions for any topic and any grade level. The important thing is to plan the questions in advance, as creating them is not something that can be done on your feet.

When you first start using good questions you might find helpful the collection of questions in Part Two, "Good Questions to Use in Math Lessons." After awhile you will want to create good questions for yourself. Detailed on pages 7 and 8 are two methods that can be used to construct good questions. The one you use is a matter of personal preference.

Method 1: Working Backward

This is a three-step process.

> Step 1: Identify a topic.
> Step 2: Think of a closed question and write down the answer.
> Step 3: Make up a question that includes (or addresses) the answer.

For example:

> Step 1: The topic for tomorrow is averages.

Step 2: The closed question might be *The children in the Smith family are aged 3, 8, 9, 10, and 15. What is their average age?* The answer is 9.

Step 3: The good question could be *There are five children in a family. Their average age is 9. How old might the children be?*

STEP 1 Identify a topic.	STEP 2 Think of an answer.	STEP 3 Make up a question that includes the answer.
rounding	11.7	My coach said that I ran 100 yards in about 12 seconds. What might the numbers on the stopwatch have been?
counting	4 chairs	I counted something in our room. There were exactly 4. What might I have counted?
area	6cm^2	How many triangles can you draw each with an area of 6cm^2?
fractions	$3\frac{1}{2}$	Two numbers are multiplied to give $3\frac{1}{2}$. What might the numbers be?
money	35 cents	I bought some things at a supermarket and got 35 cents change. What did I buy and how much did each item cost?
graphing	x x x x x x x x x x x x x x x x x 1 2 3 4 5	What could this be the graph of?

Some more examples of how this works are shown in the following table.

Method 2: Adapting a Standard Question

This is also a three-step process.

Step 1: Identify a topic.
Step 2: Think of a standard question.
Step 3: Adapt it to make a good question.

For example:

Step 1: The topic for tomorrow is measuring length using nonstandard units.

Step 2: A typical exercise might be *What is the length of your table measured in handspans?*

Step 3: The good question could be *Can you find an object that is three handspans long?*

Some more examples of how this works are shown in the following table.

STEP 1 Identify a topic.	STEP 2 Think of an standard question.	STEP 3 Adapt it to make a good question.
space	What is a square?	How many things can you write about this square?
addition	337 + 456 =	On a train trip I was working out some distances. I spilt some soft drink on my paper and some numbers disappeared. My paper looked like $\quad$ 3 ? 7 $\underline{+\ ?\ ?\ 6}$ $\quad$ 7 9 ? What might the missing numbers be?
subtraction	731 – 256 =	Arrange the digits so that the difference is between 100 and 200.
time	What is the time shown on this clock? 	What is your favorite time of day? Show it on a clock.

The more experience you have with good questions the more you will want to use them, and the easier it will become for you to make up your own. Refer to either or both of these methods until you feel confident.

3 Using Good Questions in Your Classroom

Today's mathematics classrooms should be dynamic places where children are involved and engaged in their own learning. This can be achieved through activities that promote higher level thinking, cooperative problem solving, and communication.

We have seen that good questions support these activities and are readily available for teachers to use. The first part of this section describes generally how to use a good question as the basis of a mathematics lesson. It sets out the important steps of the lesson, explains the roles of the teacher and students, and advises how to overcome problems that could arise at each stage. The second part of this section takes you through each of the steps with a specific good question.

Before the start of a lesson it is necessary to choose or create a good question. This should be aimed at the appropriate level for the children in your class. At first you might find the question you choose is too easy or too difficult, but keep practicing because you will soon get the hang of it. Once you have chosen the question then the following steps should help you to use it with your class.

Step 1: Pose the Good Question

It is a good idea to have the question written on the blackboard and as you ask the question refer to the words on the board. It is very important to make sure that all children know what the question is; do not assume they know it because it is on the board. You could even ask some students to repeat the question in their own words.

Allow some time for children to ask you about the meaning of the task. Explain the task to them if necessary but do not give any directions or suggestions on how to do it. This is for the children to work out for themselves.

Step 2: Students Work on the Good Question

When first using good questions in your classroom it is better to let the children work in pairs or small groups. This allows them to communicate their ideas to others. This communication is an important part of learning. Working together can also assist those children who may have difficulty starting. If these children have to wait for the teacher then organizational and attitudinal problems can arise.

If, once children start working, there are too many who cannot make progress without teacher assistance then it might be necessary to stop and have a whole class discussion to overcome the general concerns. If the concerns of each group, or individuals within each group, are all different then this is a sign that the question you have posed is too difficult for the class. If this happens either make the question easier or suggest that the students represent the problem in some way, such as by using materials or drawing a diagram. A variety of concrete materials should always be available for children to select from. You could also decide to abandon the question altogether as unsuitable at this stage. If this happens do not worry, as it takes time and practice to choose appropriate good questions. However, you will find good questions to be worth the effort and perseverance. Ideally, you should plan in advance how to help children who may not be able to start on the question.

Once the groups are working, your task is to monitor their progress. If a group stops after giving one response, ask them to look for other possible answers. If they have found all possible answers ask them to describe all their answers. In this way they can experience the meaning of a general solution. You could also ask a related question to extend them. For example, a related question for the task *The stopwatch shows tenths of seconds. My coach said that I ran 100 yards in about 12 seconds. What might the numbers on the stopwatch have been?* could be *What if the stopwatch showed hundredths?*

It is not vital that you wait until all groups have finished the task before initiating a discussion. They will all have answered the question to a degree. It is better to stop while students are still engaged with the question and interested in the task. This way they do not become distracted or need to be given additional work of a different type. You could give a five minute warning before you stop groups so they have time to tie up the loose ends.

Step 3: Whole Class Discussion

This is an important phase. Ask the pairs or groups in turn to suggest responses and to explain their thinking. As each does this write their responses on the blackboard or, if this is not appropriate, display their model or diagram, making sure to give each group equal status. If a response is not suitable be supportive, but try to find out the cause of the error. As we saw earlier, good questions can often make it easier for teachers to pinpoint exactly where their students are experiencing difficulty. Also, as students are explaining what they have done they often see the error for themselves anyway.

Step 4: Teacher Summary

Usually, if the task is at an appropriate level, some of the students will make the main teaching points for you during the class review. Nevertheless, just because one or more students give a response does not mean that they all understand. Thus it is necessary to summarize the discussion for everyone, emphasizing and explaining key points. Wherever possible do this using models and teaching aids. Because different people learn in different ways we need to use as wide a range of methods and materials as possible to model a situation. Also, make sure you relate the answers back to the task children have been working on so that the discussion remains meaningful. It is also helpful to pose more questions using a similar format so that the students can apply what they have learned to new situations.

An Example of a Good Question

Now let us have a look at how these steps would apply to the following good question.

Two-fifths ($\frac{2}{5}$) of the students in a school borrow books from the library each day. How many students might there be in the school and how many of them borrow books each day?

Step 1: Pose the Good Question

Have the question written on the blackboard and as you ask the question refer to the words on the board. Ask some students to read the question out loud and ask others to tell you what it means in their own words. Let children ask you any questions they may have. Explain the task to them if necessary but do not give any directions or suggestions on how to do the task. This is for the children to work out for themselves.

Step 2: Students Work on the Good Question

Organize the children to work in pairs or groups. Once they start working check that they are able to continue without teacher assistance. If necessary stop them and have a whole class discussion to overcome any general concerns. If most of the groups are finding it difficult you could make the question easier by changing the fraction to a unit fraction such as $\frac{1}{2}$, $\frac{1}{4}$, or $\frac{1}{5}$, or suggest that the groups use counters to represent the school children. If only one or two groups are finding it difficult let them start on an easier related fraction such as $\frac{1}{5}$, and when they understand this extend it to $\frac{2}{5}$.

Monitor the progress of the groups. If a group stops after giving one response, ask them to look for other possible answers. If they have found a few answers you could ask them to think of a way to describe all their answers. For example, they could look for a pattern or a rule. You could also give a related task to extend them such as *Find the pattern if $\frac{3}{5}$ of the students borrow books each day.*

When all groups have at least one response to the question give them a five minute warning and after this time stop all students. Do not be concerned that groups are at different stages.

Step 3: Whole Class Discussion

Ask the groups in turn to present their responses to the class. Some groups may want to use the counters to show their responses. Remember that students can respond at a variety of levels. For example, some possible responses are:

- It could be anything.
- One hundred students, forty of whom borrow books each day.
- The number of students in the school is a multiple of 5, such as 5, 10, 15, 20, and so on, and the number borrowing books would then be 2, 4, 6, 8, and so on.

These three responses differ not only in the level of mathematical understanding but also in the quality of thinking that is demonstrated by the answers.

Good Questions for Math Teaching

Try to take a positive approach to each group's response. For example, if the first response is given you could agree with the group and then ask them if they can give a specific answer. The group who gave the third response could be asked to demonstrate it using counters if they have not already done so.

Step 4: Teacher Summary

The main points from the activity are the pattern that emerges (2:5, 4:10, 6:15, and so on), and the use of fractions as operators (for example, $\frac{2}{5}$ of 10). Even if these points have been discussed it is important to go over them again. It would also be helpful to ask children to suggest how they would calculate $\frac{2}{5}$ of certain amounts and let them demonstrate using materials. You could also look at what happens to the answer when the amount is not a multiple of 5. As you are summarizing do not lose sight of the original question. Refer to it when necessary to make a point.

A similar task that you could pose is *In a survey I found that $\frac{3}{4}$ of the people liked Michael Jordan. How many people did I ask, and how many liked Michael Jordan?*

Thus we can see that using good questions in your classroom requires a different lesson format from a lesson in which the teacher demonstrates a technique or skill and follows up with student practice. It places different demands on a teacher, too. As well as being receptive to all students' responses, the teacher must acknowledge the validity of the various responses while making clear any limitations, drawing out contradictions or misconceptions, and building class discussion from partial answers. We have seen how good questions provide the environment for better learning; it is up to the teacher to ensure that the opportunities for learning become realities.

Good Questions to Use in Math Lessons

This section contains many good questions for you to select from and use in your classroom.

Questions are presented for sixteen mathematics topics in the areas of number, measurement, geometry, and chance and data. The questions for each topic are organized into three grade levels:

Grades K–2
Grades 3–4
Grades 5–6

For the topic of decimals, there are questions only for grades 3–4 and 5–6.

At the beginning of each level is a list of experiences that children should encounter for the particular topic. Not all children will be ready for these experiences at the same time. It is quite possible that some children in grades 3 and 4 might be working on some of the experiences listed for K–2 while other children in grades 3 and 4 are working on some of the experiences listed for grades 5 and 6. They should not be treated as a progression of experiences but rather as a range of possible experiences.

Many of the questions in these levels can be adapted to meet the needs of the students in your classroom by making them easier or more difficult.

As you are reading through the good questions that follow, you will find some instances where they have been written as investigations rather than questions. This has been done where we felt they were better written as investigations. Use them in exactly the same way as the questions.

Below each question there are teacher notes. Sometimes these are to make you aware of some important teaching points for the particular question. They may also help you ascertain if children have understood the concept being presented. At other times they will be useful in helping you assess children so you can plan to overcome any difficulties. It is a good idea to make notes as you observe children working to use in future planning.

A list of materials that you might need is provided at the beginning of each level. You will not need all of these materials unless you complete every question listed for the topic at that level. Check that you have suitable materials before you present a question to your class. It is important that children have a variety of concrete materials to select from when they are working on mathematical tasks.

4 | Number

The six topics included in this strand are:

- money
- fractions
- decimals
- place value
- counting and ordering
- operations

There are links in these number topics with the other areas of the mathematics curriculum and with each other. It is neither possible nor useful to try to treat them separately. The questions in each topic do, however, have their main teaching point within that topic.

While answering these questions children will develop a feeling for the way numbers work. They will develop number sense not only for whole numbers but also for where fractions and decimals fit into the number system. They will understand the importance of estimation and mental calculation skills and use calculators to enable them to understand key ideas without having to do complicated calculations before they are ready to do so.

Do not forget to adapt questions where necessary by making numbers or amounts smaller or larger.

Money (Grades K–2)

EXPERIENCES AT THIS LEVEL WILL HELP CHILDREN TO:

- recognize different coins
- describe, sort, and classify coins
- exchange money for goods in play situations and give appropriate change
- order money amounts
- use coins to represent written money amounts and use numbers to record the value of a group of coins
- use estimation and a calculator for money calculations

MATERIALS

- coins and play bills
- goods marked with varying prices below $1.00 as part of the class store (Ensure that there are combinations of items that add to $1.00.)

Good Questions and Teacher Notes

1. How many different ways can you make 20 cents?
2. In my pocket I have 75 cents. What coins might I have?

> In questions #1 and #2, children should realize that there are many different ways to make a money amount. See if they use only multiples of one coin, for example, four nickels, as well as combinations of different coins, for example, 10 cents + 5 cents + 5 cents.
>
> Are children confident when counting in 5s, 10s, 20s?

3. I bought something and got 5 cents change. How much did it cost and how much money did I give to pay for it?

> Children's responses might be:
>
> - costs 5 cents and gives 10 cents
> - costs 15 cents and gives 20 cents
> - costs 95 cents and gives $1.00
> - costs $1.95 and gives $2.00
>
> Can children see the folly of giving 15 cents for an item costing 10 cents to receive 5 cents change?

Good Questions for Math Teaching

4. I spent exactly $1.00 at our class shop. What might I have bought?

> Check how children add amounts to $1.00. Note if they calculate multiples of 5, 10, or 20 to make $1.00, for example, do they know five items at 10 cents each is 50 cents or do they add each one separately?

5. I am a coin with a building on me. What might I be?

> The main focus here is to look more closely at the attributes of coins.

6. I have two coins in one hand and one in the other hand. The coins in each hand are worth the same amount. What could the coins be?

> Note if children develop a system when recording. How easily do they calculate amounts?

7. The answer to a calculation is 35 cents. What is the question? Refer to this list to help you.

CAFETERIA PRICE LIST

Peanut butter sandwich	$1.10	Salad	$1.55
Ham & salad roll	$1.40	Bag of chips	$ .65
Fruit salad	$1.15	Piece of fruit	$ .20
Cookie	$ .15		

> Can children write more than one question?

8. I had one of each of the coins in our currency on my table. I sorted them into two groups. What might the groups have been?

> It is interesting to note what categories children use. Ask them to tell you their categories; don't assume you know their reasoning.

9. The price tag on a toy car is $2.75. What coins would I use to pay for this?

> Note if children develop a system when recording. How easily do they calculate amounts?

10. I have exactly $100 in bills in my pocket. What bills might I have?

> Are children aware of available bills? Check if they can count in 5s, 10s, 20s, 50s.

11. Someone was asked to remember the cost of five items. They knew the most expensive was $2.00 and the least expensive was 50 cents. What might the other three be?

> The focus here is on ordering of money amounts. Note if the children can record different amounts correctly.

Money (Grades 3–4)

EXPERIENCES AT THIS LEVEL WILL HELP CHILDREN TO:

- ■ round to the nearest dollar to estimate or check total cost
- ■ record money amounts
- ■ pay with appropriate amounts when the exact amount is not available
- ■ order money amounts
- ■ use an appropriate method (mental, written, calculator) to solve problems involving money

MATERIALS

- ■ coins and play bills
- ■ supermarket advertisements from newspapers
- ■ calculators

Good Questions and Teacher Notes

1. I bought an item at a shop and got 35 cents change. What did I buy and how much did it cost?

> Children need to see the folly of including such things as buying an item costing 5 cents and giving 40 cents to get 35 cents change. Note if children look for a pattern when recording answers.

2. I gave change of $1.00 using quarters, dimes, and nickels. What might the change have looked like?

> Note if children record systematically and accurately. Check how easily they make $1.00.

3. How could I spend exactly $20.00 at the supermarket? (Use a supermarket advertisement and a calculator to help.)

> Check if children use estimation skills to help them; for example, they might

round off some amounts to assist their estimation. Note how they use the calculator.

4. In my pocket I have $36.00. What bills might I have?

This allows you to see how familiar children are with the various bills and if they use a system when recording.

5. I spent $60.00 on six tickets to the theater. How many adults and children are there and how much are the tickets?

Are the answers realistic? Can children multiply amounts, for example, 4 x $10 or 4 x $5? Note if they figure mentally or use paper and pencil to compute.

6. When I was in a music shop I saw that a CD cost about $22 and a tape about $15. What might have been the price tag on the CD and the tape?

This question focuses on rounding off. Are children aware that they can round up and down?

7. A number sentence uses three of the following amounts or numbers: $1.50, 2, $3.75, 50 cents, 6, $3.00, 75 cents. What might the number sentence be?

The main focus here is to see if children use a variety of processes, for example, 6 x .50 = $3, $1.50 ÷ 2 = .75, $3.75 − .75 = $3.00.

8. My friends and I shared an amount of money equally between us. We each got $1.20. How much money was there and how many friends might I have?

It is interesting to see how children do this—mentally, with paper and pencil, or with coins. When they check their answer do they include themselves or only the friends?

9. I bought something and paid for it with three coins. What might it have been and how much did it cost?

Look for a range of responses that are realistic.

10. I went to get $100 out of the bank. What are the different ways I can ask for this amount of bills?

Note how children multiply and divide by 2, 5, 10, and 20.

23 ■ I I   Number

Money (Grades 5–6)

EXPERIENCES AT THIS LEVEL WILL HELP CHILDREN TO:

- use mental calculation and estimation
- use +, −, x, and ÷ for written computation of money
- select an appropriate operation to solve problems involving money

MATERIALS

- play money, notes, and coins
- new and used car section of a newspaper
- calculators

Good Questions and Teacher Notes

1. Scientific calculators cost $20.00 and basic calculators cost $5.00. How much might it cost for a class set of some basic and some scientific calculators?

> Note how children decide how many of each calculator to purchase. Do they record their answers systematically? Do they choose appropriate operations to work out the price? How easily do they handle these operations?

2. I have $25,000 and want to buy two cars. What could I buy?

> Note if children can justify their answers and if they can provide a range of answers.

3. If one of the bills currently in use was to be changed to a coin, which one would you choose? Why?

> Children should be able to justify their choice in a reasonable manner. You could extend this by looking at bills and coins in use in other countries.

4. You are spending five nights away. You have won $500 for accommodations. Where could you stay?

Top class hotel	$300 per night
4 star hotel	$225 " "
3 star hotel	$100 " "
2 star hotel	$60 " "
Backpackers	$25 " "

Note what methods children use to work this out, that is, do they readily multiply amounts when needed or do they always add amounts? They can stay at different places.

5. Design a rounding policy for a supermarket.

The way children approach this will tell you if they understand rounding. It is interesting to note whose side they are on—owner or customer?

Fractions (Grades K–2)

EXPERIENCES AT THIS LEVEL WILL HELP CHILDREN TO:
- use informal fraction language for objects and collections
- compare fractional parts of objects and collections

MATERIALS
- fraction materials such as rods, counters, or shapes
- lengths of string, tape, or yarn

Good Questions and Teacher Notes

1. You see a sign in a shop window that reads $\frac{1}{2}$ OFF SALE. What does this mean to you?

Listen carefully to children's responses as these will indicate the depth of their understanding. Also, give them some prices, ask them how much the sale price would be, and ask them to explain their reasoning.

2. Half of the people in a family are males. What might a drawing of the family look like?

Do children understand that there must be the same number of people in each group? Make sure they see a range of drawings done by class members.

3. Draw a shape. Show how to cut the shape into two halves.

Do children show equal parts?

4. I was listening to the radio and I heard the announcer say "half." What might she have been referring to?

The answers will indicate depth of understanding. Two possible responses are "Half-past 3" and "Half-time."

5. We want to paint the top half of the room. How could we find out where the half-way mark is?

Allow children to do this how they want but have some string, tape, and so on, available for their use. The main focus here is to look at how practical the children's strategies are.

6. What do you know and what can you find out about $\frac{1}{4}$? Record it on paper or show it with materials.

Note if children understand $\frac{1}{4}$ as part of a whole and as part of a collection. Can they use a range of materials to represent it?

Fractions (Grades 3–4)

EXPERIENCES AT THIS LEVEL WILL HELP CHILDREN TO:
- represent simple fractional parts of objects and collections
- order and compare fractions with the same denominators
- write common fractions
- record simple equivalence, for example, $\frac{1}{2} = \frac{2}{4} = \frac{3}{6}$
- add and subtract tenths and fractions with like denominators

MATERIALS
- concrete materials, for example, counters, shapes, or rods
- drawing paper for designs, such as origami or other square paper
- circles cut into quarters to represent "pizzas"

Good Questions and Teacher Notes

1. How many different designs can you make that are $\frac{3}{4}$ red and $\frac{1}{4}$ yellow?

Note if the designs are simple or complex. Ask children to explain how they know $\frac{3}{4}$ is red and $\frac{1}{4}$ is yellow.

2. One-third of a class orders lunches from the cafeteria each day. How many students might be in the class and how many of them order lunches each day?

Let children use counters to represent the students if they wish. Can they find more than one answer? Do they base their answers on multiples of 3?

Good Questions for Math Teaching

3. My aunt said that when she was half her age she could touch her toes. How old might she be now and how old was she when she could touch her toes?

> Check that suggested answers are realistic.

4. I picked up a handful of M&M's. One-third of them were red. What might a drawing of the M&M's look like?

> This requires children to show a fractional part of a collection. Do children provide a range of answers and does anyone develop a system to do so? Do children understand why amounts that are not multiples of 3 do not work?

5. I had some pizzas that I cut into quarters. How many pizzas might I have had, and how many quarters might I have after cutting them?

> Can children identify a relationship between wholes and quarters?

6. How many different ways can you show $\frac{2}{3}$?

> Note if children understand $\frac{2}{3}$ as part of a whole or part of a length and as part of a collection. Do they use a range of materials to represent it?

7. I folded an origami square to show a fraction. How did I fold it and what might the fraction have been?

> Look for equal parts and a range of answers.

8. A friend of mine put these fractions into two groups: $\frac{3}{4}, \frac{2}{5}, \frac{1}{3}, \frac{6}{10}, \frac{1}{10}$. What might the two groups be?

> Ask children to give reasons for their groups as these could highlight some misconceptions. One possible grouping is to put $\frac{1}{3}$ and $\frac{1}{10}$ in one group because they are unit fractions; another grouping is to put $\frac{3}{4}$ and $\frac{6}{10}$ in one group because they are greater than $\frac{1}{2}$.

Fractions (Grades 5–6)

EXPERIENCES AT THIS LEVEL WILL HELP CHILDREN TO:
- use equivalence to compare and order fractions
- locate fractions on a number line
- rename fractions in different forms, for example, as percentages or decimals

- mentally add and subtract common equivalent fractions
- add and subtract fractions with related denominators
- understand the relationship between division and fractions

MATERIALS

- fraction materials, for example, counters, shapes, rods, or kits

Good Questions and Teacher Notes

1. Two fractions add up to $\frac{1}{2}$. What might those two fractions be?

Do children only use known fraction combinations such as $\frac{1}{4} + \frac{1}{4}$ or do they use subtraction to find other possibilities, for example, $\frac{1}{2} - \frac{1}{3} = \frac{1}{6}$, so $\frac{1}{3} + \frac{1}{6} = \frac{1}{2}$? Do they use equivalence, for example, $\frac{1}{2} = \frac{6}{12}$, so $\frac{1}{12} + \frac{5}{12} = \frac{1}{2}$

2. Some numbers add up to 10. I know that at least one of them has a fraction part in it, but none uses decimals. What might the numbers be?

As above, note the methods children use to find answers. These will tell you a lot about their understanding of fractions.

3. What three fractions might I add together and get an answer of $\frac{1}{2}$?

Again look at the methods used. Do children guess and then work it out to check? If so, how do they then adjust the fractions? Do they know which fractions are smaller than $\frac{1}{2}$?

4. The answer is $\frac{3}{7}$. What might the question be?

Encourage children to use other processes than just addition.

5. What two fractions might I subtract to get an answer of $\frac{3}{4}$?

Do children use equivalence ("I know $\frac{3}{4} = \frac{6}{8}$, so $\frac{7}{8} - \frac{1}{8} = \frac{3}{4}$") or some other method to do this?

6. $\frac{1}{?} \times 3? = 1?$. What might the missing numbers be?

The missing numbers do not have to be the same. Can children describe all of the answers? Can they prove they have all of the answers? (There are nine possibilities.)

7. A rectangle has a perimeter of two units. What might the area be?

> Yes, this is a fraction question! The perimeter must be a combination of fractions, for example, $\frac{1}{2} + \frac{1}{2} + \frac{1}{2} + \frac{1}{2}$, $\frac{1}{4} + \frac{3}{4} + \frac{1}{4} + \frac{3}{4}$, and so on. The area will vary depending on the length of the sides. You may want to remind the students that a square is a rectangle.

8. Write some different stories about $3 \div \frac{1}{2}$.

> The purpose of this is for children to understand the difference between $3 \div \frac{1}{2}$ and $\frac{1}{2}$ of 3. Their stories will indicate this. Stories like "I had \$3.00 and I gave half to my friend" are *not* appropriate.

9. *Teacher:* "Which is bigger, $\frac{201}{301}$ or $\frac{2}{3}$?" *Student:* "$\frac{201}{301}$ is bigger because 1 has been added to the top and the bottom." Is this reasoning correct? Are there any examples where adding 1 to the top and the bottom makes the fraction bigger?

> This question highlights a misconception that some children may have.

10. $\frac{?}{?} < \frac{3}{4}$. What might the missing fraction be?

> Provide concrete materials for this question. Do not assume that because some children write, for example, $\frac{1}{3}$ that their understanding is correct. Check why they write this. Some children may think any number smaller than the 3 or the 4 will make a smaller fraction and will not consider fractions such as $\frac{1}{5}$, $\frac{5}{10}$, and so on, to be smaller. This question checks the same misconception as question 9.

Decimals (Grades 3–4)

EXPERIENCES AT THIS LEVEL WILL HELP CHILDREN TO:
- read decimals on a calculator screen
- write decimal numerals
- round off to nearest whole number
- record and order numbers with two decimal places
- add and subtract numbers involving tenths
- understand how decimals fit in the number system

MATERIALS
- calculators
- materials to model decimals, for example, base 10 materials, Popsicle sticks, interlocking cubes, or metric rulers

Good Questions and Teacher Notes

1. A decimal number has been rounded off to 6. What might the number be?

> This will establish if children understand the concept of rounding. Do they give one number or do they know it can include 5.5 but must be smaller than 6.5?

2. I am thinking of some decimal numbers between 1 and 2. What might they be? Give at least 15 answers.

3. My big sister says that the 100-yard record at her school is between 12 and 13 seconds. What might the record be?

> In questions #2 and #3, note which children give answers using only hundredths or only tenths and which children give a combination of these. Are there any children who include thousandths? Does anyone give the complete range of tenths and hundredths?

4. Using only these keys on your calculator (5, ., 4, +, =), what numbers can you make the calculator show?

> Children should use a range of processes. Note how comfortable they are with the functioning of the calculator.

5. Represent 1.4 with materials in at least five different ways.

> Provide plenty of concrete materials for this question. Some you might find useful are base 10 blocks, Popsicle sticks, metric rulers, interlocking cubes, and play money.

6. I added three decimal numbers together to make exactly 4. What might the three numbers be?

> Look for a variety of answers. Do children add two of them and then subtract from 4 to find the third?

7. If I use a *flat* to represent one whole, a *long* to represent tenths, and a unit to represent hundredths what numbers can I represent using exactly ten pieces?

> Children need to work with base 10 blocks to do this question. You could extend it by asking them to show the biggest or smallest possible number using ten pieces.

8. In this number sentence, what might the missing digits be? 2 < ?.?

> Can children give the entire range (2.1 to 9.9, including numbers like 5.0)?

Good Questions for Math Teaching

Decimals (Grades 5–6)

EXPERIENCES AT THIS LEVEL WILL HELP CHILDREN TO:

■ read, write, and order decimals to three places
■ round off to the nearest whole number and use this skill to estimate
■ rename common fractions as decimals and vice versa
■ select and use appropriate operations to deal with decimals

MATERIALS

■ calculators
■ metric rulers
■ strips of card or paper

Good Questions and Teacher Notes

1. How many different ways can you make your calculator show a number with a particular decimal such as 12.34 without pressing the decimal point button?

> Some possible answers are 1234 ÷ 100; 1234 ÷ 10 ÷ 10; 2468 ÷ 200; 617 ÷ 50; 1234 x 1 percent (if available).

2. Two numbers each with four digits are added and the result is rounded off to 2.7. What might those numbers be?

> The two numbers must total in the range 2.650 to 2.749 to be rounded off to 2.7. Do any children think about this relationship before trying to find the two numbers?

3. In this calculation some numbers are missing. What might they be?

$$\begin{array}{r} 3.?? \\ +\,?.7? \\ \hline 6.?3 \end{array}$$

> Do children give more than one answer and do they record their answers systematically? Do they realize that ten different digits can go on the top line?

4. I wrote a sequence of numbers, adding the same number to each to get the next number. I wrote down 2.57 to start and 3.61 to finish. What might the numbers in between be?

The children could count by 0.02, 0.04, 0.08, or 0.26. Note which of them use a calculator to assist them to work this out. Do any children find the difference between 3.61 and 2.57 (1.04) and then find out which numbers divide evenly into it?

5. 3. ?1 + ?.47 + 0.? = 8.68. What might the missing numbers be?

Note how children do this. Who does it by trial and error? Who develops a system such as deciding on one of the numbers and then subtracting it from 8.68 to see what is left to work with?

6. Two numbers multiply together to give 14.4. What might these numbers be?

It is useful if children have calculators to help with this one. Do they divide 14.4 by various numbers to find a solution, for example, 14.4 ÷ 2.5 = 5.76, so 5.76 x 2.5 = 14.4?

7. What numbers could be rounded off to 5.8?

This gives children a different way to think about rounding and emphasizes the significance of place value. The numbers can include or be bigger than 5.75 but must be less than 5.85. Most children can give one number that can be rounded. If they can give the entire range it shows they have a complete understanding of the concept of rounding.

8. In a race the times are measured to hundredths of a second. The winner's time is 12.52 seconds. What might the times of the other eight runners be?

The main point is to check if children are able to order decimals. Note how realistic the times are. The times of the other runners must be greater than 12.52, for example, 12.53, 13.27, and so on.

9. ?.? x ?.?= ?.?. What might the missing numbers be? Use a calculator to help you.

Do children try to do this by trial and error or do they know that they must multiply numbers with 0.2 and 0.5 to get a result with only tenths not hundredths? Some possible answers are 1.2 x 1.5 = 1.8, 1.2 x 3.5 = 4.2 … 1.2 x 6.5 = 7.8; 2.2 x 1.5 = 3.3, 2.2 x 2.5 = 5.5 … 2.2 x 4.5 = 9.9, and so on. It is important to see the pattern if you want to find all possible answers.

10. I divided 6.12 by 3 and wrote down the answer, 2.4. What did I do wrong and what other similar questions might I get wrong?

It is a common mistake for children to leave out the zero in such examples. If they are able to give other examples then they are aware of the error.

11. I multiplied two decimal numbers on a calculator and got a whole number answer. What might the two decimal numbers have been?

This is similar to the previous question. The answer will have at least two zeros at the end, which have been "dropped off" by the calculator.

12. How can you work out a way to get the answer for 3.5 ÷ 4 without pressing the 5 button on your calculator?

Help each child explain their strategy and what it means. The answer is 0.875. One way of doing it is to do 3.6 ÷ 4 = 0.9 and then subtract the result of 0.1 ÷ 4 (0.25) from 0.9 to make 0.875.

Place Value (Grades K–2)

EXPERIENCES AT THIS LEVEL WILL HELP CHILDREN TO:
- recognize, order, and write up to three-digit numbers
- develop early rounding ideas to 10
- recognize zero as a number
- group items in tens to count larger collections
- use place value to work with patterns on a hundreds number chart

MATERIALS
- base 10 materials
- a hundreds chart

Good Questions and Teacher Notes

1. What numbers can you make that are below 100 and have 6 in the tens place?

This will indicate if children understand that the value of a digit depends on its position within a number.

2. I am thinking of a number between 10 and 100 with a single 9 in it. What might my number be?

Note if children are able to find all possible answers. Ask them how they can tell if they have them all.

3. What do you know and what can you find out about the number 180?

> Accept any suitable responses. Question further any children who do not include a response that shows their awareness of place value, for example, 180 is 100 + 80, or 18 groups of 10, and so on.

4. What numbers can you make using 6, 5, and 8?

> Do children record their answers systematically and know when they have recorded all possibilities? Do any children include single digits, for example, 5, as one of their answers?

5. A two-digit number contains exactly one 4. What might the number be?

> It is important to present the answers succinctly. How many different numbers might there be?

6. How many different ways can you make the number 20 adding only the numbers 10 and 1? You may use each of these numbers as many times as you wish or not at all.

> This question helps children to see that 20 can be named in many ways.

7. Using base 10 materials how many ways can you show the number 25?

> After finding different ways, ask children which way uses the fewest number of blocks.

Place Value (Grades 3–4)

EXPERIENCES AT THIS LEVEL WILL HELP CHILDREN TO:
- order and write whole numbers to the thousands and decimals to two places
- round to 10, 100, 1,000, or 10,000 for estimation
- extend multiplication facts using place value, for example, 3 x 5 = 15, so 3 x 5 tens = 15 tens
- use place value to explain number patterns

MATERIALS
- price catalogs
- base 10 materials
- a hundreds chart

Good Questions and Teacher Notes

1. A number has been rounded off to 1,200. What might the number be?

> This depends on whether it has been rounded off to the nearest 10 or nearest 100. Numbers from 1,195 to 1,204 would round off to 1,200 as the nearest 10, or numbers from 1,150 to 1,249 would round off to 1,200 as the nearest 100.

2. How many numbers can you write with 8 in the hundreds place?

> Note if children only write numbers starting with 800 or if they write numbers above 1,000.

3. How many numbers can you make using the digits 1, 2, 3, and 4? You can only use each digit once in each number.

> Do children record their answers systematically and know when they have recorded all possibilities?

4. How many articles/items can you find in a catalog with prices that have a 1 in the units place and a 9 in the tenths place?

> To do this children have to be able to recognize the units and tenths places within larger numbers, for example, $21.95, $1.90, and so on.

5. How many ways can you rename 1,265 as the sum of smaller numbers?

> How confident are children when moving between 1,000s, 100s, 10s, and ones? Two possible answers are 1,000 + 200 + 60 + 5; 1,000 + 100 + 150 + 15.

6. Two numbers multiply to make 360. One of them has a zero on the end. What might the two numbers be?

> Can children find all possibilities? Can they see the pattern between pairs of numbers?

7. An easy way to add 9 is to add 10 and take away 1. Using a similar strategy what other numbers might I add or subtract in this way?

> Children should be able to use other strategies such as to add 11 and 10 and then add 1 more; to subtract 99 take away 100 and add 1; and so on.

8. I wrote down a number with one zero in it, but I cannot remember what it was. I know it was between 500 and 800. What might it have been?

Can children find all possible answers? How do they know they have found them all?

Place Value (Grades 5–6)

EXPERIENCES AT THIS LEVEL WILL HELP CHILDREN TO:
- compare and order large numbers and decimals to thousandths
- round numbers for estimation purposes

MATERIALS
- materials to model numbers

Good Questions and Teacher Notes

1. What numbers can you make using 1, 0, 2, 7, 8, and 4?

    Children should record their answers methodically. You could ask them to write down the largest or smallest number it is possible to make using all the digits.

2. Represent 247 in as many different ways as you can, with materials and numbers.

    Variety is important here. Have materials available for children to use. Do they use systems that take advantage of place value?

3. Two numbers multiply to give 36,000. What might the two numbers be?

    Yes, this is a place value question! The key aspect is the zeros. Note how children handle them.

Counting and Ordering (Grades K–2)

EXPERIENCES AT THIS LEVEL WILL HELP CHILDREN TO:
- compare and order using one-to-one correspondence
- write, say, and count numbers to ten and beyond
- skip count forward and backward (ones, twos, fives, and tens to one hundred, and tens and hundreds to one thousand)
- use ordinal numbers up to ten
- recognize odd and even numbers

MATERIALS
- number charts
- interlocking cubes

Good Questions and Teacher Notes

1. Write down everything you can about the number 12.

> Not only can you see what the children know but they can become aware of what they themselves know. Repeat for other numbers.

2. Write down some odd numbers between 0 and 100.

> Check that all numbers the children write are odd. Do they record them haphazardly or methodically?

3. I have written a secret number between 50 and 70. It is an even number. What might it be?

> Can children write them all? Repeat for other numbers.

4. Make a two-color train with interlocking cubes, using two of one color, two of the other, continuing for as long as you like. How many cubes are in your train?

> Repeat for three colors. Or, ask children to build trains with three of each color.

5. I have written a secret number that is more than sixty-five. What might it be?

> Extend this by asking children to write the biggest number they can. Compare these numbers to see which is the biggest. Repeat for other numbers.

6. Count by twos until you land on twenty. What other numbers can you count by and still land on twenty?

> Repeat by increasing the goal number from twenty to fifty, then one hundred.

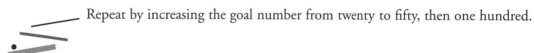

Counting and Ordering (Grades 3–4)

EXPERIENCES AT THIS LEVEL WILL HELP CHILDREN TO:
- read and write whole numbers
- skip count forward and backward by numbers from 2 to 10, starting from any number
- use materials to produce number sequences, for example, square numbers
- produce and describe number patterns
- recognize patterns in multiplication tables

MATERIALS
■ number charts
■ calculators (useful for checking or producing number patterns)

Good Questions and Teacher Notes

1. Which number in this group does not belong? Why?

15   2   8   13   16

Children must explain their responses. Their answers can differ. Are their explanations coherent?

2. What do you know and what can you find out about the multiples of 3—3, 6, 9, 12, 15, 18, 21 . . . ?

One response could be that the sums of the digits of the multiples of 3 are multiples of 3.

3. Create a skip counting pattern starting at 91 that someone else can continue.

It is important that children can describe their pattern to others. They could check each other's.

4. I doubled a number and kept doubling so that the original number was doubled four times. What might the answer be?

The answer will be a multiple of 16 (16, 32, 48 . . .). Do children use all the information in the question?

5. Starting at zero, what numbers can I skip count by and land on one hundred?

Ask children to explain their results.

6. A number was shown as a set of dots. Part of the pattern looks like

What might the number be? How do you know?

Accept any reasonable answers as long as children can justify them.

7. My father is double my age. How old might I be?

8. My dog is half as old as me. How old might I be and how old is the dog?

9. My dog is half as old as me. My mother is double my age. How old might we each be?

For questions #7, #8, and #9, the ages should be within a practical range. For example, in question #9 ages of 2 (dog), 4 (me), and 8 (my mother) or 4 (dog), 8 (me), and 16 (my mother) are not acceptable. Note if children develop systems based on the inherent patterns to find responses.

Counting and Ordering (Grades 5–6)

EXPERIENCES AT THIS LEVEL WILL HELP CHILDREN TO:

■ count beyond one thousand starting from any number
■ continue, create, and describe sequences of fractions and decimals
■ continue, create, and describe sequences involving constant multiplication and division or combinations of operations
■ identify and work with prime numbers

MATERIALS

■ number charts
■ calculators (useful for checking or producing number patterns)

Good Questions and Teacher Notes

1. Three consecutive even numbers add up to a number between 100 and 120. What might the numbers be?

Note how concisely children can communicate their answers. It is interesting to listen to them tell how they got their answers.

2. I am thinking of a number. The hundreds digit is larger than the ones digit. The tens digit is larger than the hundreds and it is odd. What might my number be?

Do children use all of the information to get an answer? Note if they check their answer against the question.

3. Create a skip counting pattern starting at 2.05 that someone else can continue.

Are children able to describe their pattern? How sophisticated are the responses? Let them check each other's patterns.

4. I am thinking of a number. If I divide by 3 there is a remainder of 1. If I divide by 4 there is a remainder of 1. What might my number be?

> The pattern is key in this question. Are children able to describe it?

5. I halved a number and kept halving for a total of five times. The answer was a whole number. What number might I have started with?

> It will be an even number and a multiple of 32. Ask children to describe how they found an answer.

6. If I count by twos, I will land on both 100 and 1,000. If I count by threes, I won't land on either. What can you count by so that you don't land on 100 but you do land on 1,000? What can you count by to land on both 100 and 1,000?

> Note the methods children use to investigate these patterns.

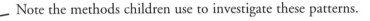

Operations (Grades K–2)

EXPERIENCES AT THIS LEVEL WILL HELP CHILDREN TO:
- use materials to explore how numbers can be decomposed
- learn about strategies for addition, for example, using doubles, counting on, and so on
- add and subtract small numbers in story problems
- write number sentences and make up stories about number sentences

MATERIALS
- counters
- toy vehicles (with different numbers of wheels)

Good Questions and Teacher Notes

1. A basketball player scored 9 points in two games. What might her scores in each of the games be?
2. ? + ? + ? = 13. What might the missing numbers be?

> The purpose of questions #1 and #2 is for children to think about the addition process in a different way and to show that there can be a range of possible answers to a given problem.

3. There are now four chickens in Mrs. Farmer's pen. How many chickens did she once have, and what happened to them?

> Note the children who use larger numbers confidently. It is important to use counters or similar aids.

4. Make up some different ways to add 5 to 8 in your head. In how many ways can you do it?

> This is to show that there is not only one correct way to do a calculation.

5. The difference between two numbers is 5. What might the two numbers be?

> This focuses on *difference* as subtraction. Some children will feel confident using larger numbers. Some may record their answers systematically, for example, 6 − 1, 7 − 2, 8 − 3, 9 − 4, and so on.

6. Yesterday I put some counters into groups with the same number in each group. I cannot remember the groups, but I can remember that there were twelve counters. What might the groups have been?

> Children need counters to do this. The possibilities are two groups of 6, three groups of 4, four groups of 3, or six groups of 2.

7. When the children in a class each got a partner, there was one child left over. How many children might there be in the class?

> This would be good to model with the class.

Operations (Grades 3–4)

EXPERIENCES AT THIS LEVEL WILL HELP CHILDREN TO:
- build on known number facts and use extended number facts
- double and halve
- develop mental strategies and estimation skills
- refine methods for addition and subtraction
- record simple multiplication and division calculations
- select the appropriate operations to solve whole number problems

MATERIALS
- counters
- base 10 materials

Good Questions and Teacher Notes

1. Make up some different ways to add 9 to 23 in your head. In how many ways can you do it?

> This is to show that there is not only one correct way to do a calculation.

2. Five numbers added together make an odd number. What do you know about the numbers?

> Either one, three, or five of the numbers must be odd. This question highlights some features of odd and even numbers.

3. What might the missing numbers be?

$$
\begin{array}{r}
3\ ? \\
+\ 1\ ? \\
\hline
?\ 2
\end{array}
$$

> This is to show that there are many possible answers. You could ask children to find all possibilities. Note those children who have difficulty working out solutions with trading.

4. The faces of this cube are numbered consecutively. What might the sum of the faces be?

> The faces we cannot see could be numbered 10, 11, and 12 or 4, 5, and 6, or in between, so the sum could be 39, 45, 51, or 57. Let children use a calculator to add the numbers. You will need to discuss what *consecutively* means.

5. I have some marbles. I give some away to my friends and am left with fifteen. How many marbles might I have started with and how many might I have given away?

> Again, look for a range of answers. Note the size of the numbers children are confident working with.

6. Eighteen people said they wanted to do folk dances. The teacher said they must dance in groups, but no one must be left out. How many different types of groups can you make?

> This is the same principle as question #6 in the previous section. Let children use counters to represent the dancers.

Operations (Grades 5–6)

EXPERIENCES AT THIS LEVEL WILL HELP CHILDREN TO:
- recall multiplication and division facts up to and including 10 x 10
- choose and use mental strategies
- estimate and check reasonableness of answers
- refine methods for addition and subtraction of whole numbers and decimals
- use suitable written methods for multiplication and division
- select the appropriate operations to solve number problems

MATERIALS
- calculators
- concrete materials where necessary

Good Questions and Teacher Notes

1. The answer to a division question is 5. What might the question be?

> Note how children do this. Do they know that if they multiply 5 by any number they will find the numbers to make their question, for example, 5 x 20 = 100, so 100 ÷ 20 = 5?

2. Using all of the digits 9, 8, 7, 6, 5, 4, 3, 2, 1 and any operations, what numbers can you make?

> Children could also be asked to find the largest or smallest number they can make.

3. I did a subtraction problem last night but can only remember the answer and that it looked like this:

$$
\begin{array}{r}
?\ ?\ ? \\
-\ ?\ ?\ ? \\
\hline
5\ 7
\end{array}
$$

What might the missing numbers be? Try to describe all possible answers.

> This question focuses on the difference between numbers. The smallest possible top number is 157 − 100 = 57 and the largest is 999 − 942 = 57. There are 843 possible combinations.

4. A school has 400 students. They all come to school by bus, and each bus carries the same number of students. How many students might there be on each bus?

> Note the methods children use to do this. Do they use division or multiplication?

5. ? x ? = 2,280. What might the missing numbers be? How many different answers can you find?

> Again, which children do this by division and which do it by trial and error multiplication? Do they use estimation skills?

6. (a) How could you calculate 23 x 4 if the 4 button on your calculator is broken? (b) How could you calculate 23 x 21 if the 2 button on your calculator is broken?

> For (a) the children could press 23 + = = = = or 23 + 23 + 23 + 23 =. For (b) they could press 13 + = = = (21 times), then add 10 (21 times).
>
> This is quite a difficult task but it provides a rich investigation.

7. Eighty-four children in four grades are arranged into teams with the same number on each team. How many teams are there and how many children might there be on each team?

> Note the methods children use to do this. Do they use division or multiplication? Do they use known number facts?

8. Write a word problem where the answer is $27\frac{1}{4}$. Write a word problem where the answer is 27 and 1 remainder.

> Are children able to deal with remainders in a sensible manner and know when to convert them to fractions and when to leave them as remainders? For example, if you share 109 pizzas among four families each family would get 27 whole pizzas and the remaining one could be cut into quarters. If you are putting 109 people on four buses you would put 27 people on each bus and fit the remaining person on one of the buses.

9. What could you add to 361 to make it divisible by 10?

Adding 9 is the obvious answer, but there are many other possible solutions. Can children find a rule for this one?

10. Using four 4s and any operation, how many different answers can you make?

It is possible to make all numbers between 1 and 100!

5 Measurement

The five topics included in this strand are:

1. weight
2. volume and capacity
3. area
4. time
5. length and perimeter

We use measurement in most aspects of our daily lives, whether it be to estimate, interpret or measure quantities accurately.

The children's experiences in answering these questions will enable them to develop an understanding of the importance of measurement while becoming familiar with the various concepts involved.

They will understand the need for more precise measurements and be able to choose appropriate units and instruments for their measuring. They will recognize situations where a reasonable estimate is more appropriate than an exact measurement.

You will find many links between the various topics. However, as in the number strand, the questions within each topic have their main teaching point within that topic. You can adapt questions by changing the amounts or quantities to suit the children in your class.

Weight (Grades K–2)

EXPERIENCES AT THIS LEVEL WILL HELP CHILDREN TO:
- use suitable language of comparison for weight, for example, heavier, lighter, too heavy, too light
- make estimates based on child's own capability to lift, pull, push, and so on
- estimate order and compare weights by feel and by a pan balance
- choose appropriate attributes for ordering
- work to improve judgments of weight

MATERIALS
- a pen, a small bucket of water, a book, a potato, a lunchbox, bottle tops, jars, rice, and various other objects
- a pan balance

Good Questions and Teacher Notes

1. What can you find that is lighter than a pen?
2. Find something that you can lift that is heavier than this bucket of water.

> Questions #1 and #2 focus on language and comparing by lifting. It is important that children get the opportunity to talk about what they did.

3. A book is on one side of a pan balance, and two objects are on the other side so the pans are level. What might the two objects be?

> Children need a pan balance to do this. Do they realize that different books have different weights?

4. What can you find that is bigger than a potato but lighter than it?
5. What can you find that is heavy but small?
6. Lin carried a big, full bucket quite easily. What might have been in the bucket?

> Questions #4, #5, and #6 require children to focus on the two attributes of weight and size. Again, the language used, both by themselves and the teacher, is essential to the development of concepts of measurement.

7. Using a pan balance I balanced my lunch box with some bottle tops, but I cannot remember how many. How many might I have used?

> Answers will vary depending on what type of lunch box you use and what is in

Good Questions for Math Teaching

it. They also depend on the bottle tops used. Note children who are aware of these variations.

8. André carried an object in a bag. When he put another object the same as the first object into the bag he could not lift it without struggling. What might the objects be?

Note if children make reasonable suggestions.

9. What objects can you find in your home that have *1 pound* marked on them? Ask someone at home to help you make a list.

Allow the children to report on what they found.

10. Fill a small jar with rice. Now find another container and fill it with water so it is the same weight as the jar with rice.

Children should see that objects that have different size, shape, and texture can have the same weight.

Weight (Grades 3–4)

EXPERIENCES AT THIS LEVEL WILL HELP CHILDREN TO:
- use direct and indirect comparison to compare and measure weight
- recognize the need for common units when direct comparisons are impossible
- choose appropriate uniform units to measure and compare
- make and improve estimates

MATERIALS
- pan balances
- various objects for weight activities
- weights, for example, objects that weigh 1 pound
- coins

Good Questions and Teacher Notes

1. Can you find two objects that have the same size but different weights?
2. Can you find two objects that have the same weight but different size?

Questions #1 and #2 focus on two attributes: size and weight. Are there any children who cannot distinguish them?

Measurement

3. I can see an object that weighs more than 1 pound but less than 2 pounds. What might the object be?

> Do children choose suitable objects to measure? Do they have a good idea of what one pound might feel and look like?

4. On each side of a balance scale I have some different coins. They balance exactly. What might the coins be?

> Do children assume that two nickels will balance one dime, two dimes and a nickel will balance one quarter, and so on?

5. I weighed one item and found that it was between $\frac{3}{4}$ pound and 1 pound. What might the item have been?

> What do children use as their 1 pound measure? How close are their choices of item?

Weight (Grades 5–6)

EXPERIENCES AT THIS LEVEL WILL HELP CHILDREN TO:
- choose and use appropriate standard units and instruments when measuring and comparing objects
- recognize that a smaller unit will give a more accurate measurement
- read scales accurately
- estimate by using known weights of objects and standard measures

MATERIALS
- scales
- spring scale
- various objects, some with a weight less than 1 pound and some between 1 pound and 2 pounds
- marbles, fruit, a small bucket

Good Questions and Teacher Notes

1. Debbie weighed a bag of flour and found it to be $5\frac{1}{4}$ pounds. Pedro weighed the same bag and found it to be $5\frac{1}{2}$ pounds. How could this happen if they had used a balance scale? How could this happen if they had used a spring scale?

> The balance scale may not have been level; some flour might have leaked; the flour might have been unevenly placed. For the spring scale there can be zero errors, reading errors, or inaccurate scales.

2. Can you find a collection of objects with a total weight of 5 pounds?

> Check how easily children can convert ounces to pounds. Do they choose objects whose weights are near to the desired weight?

3. A jar of marbles weighs 1 pound. How much might each marble weigh? How much might the jar weigh?

> Note how children work this out. Do they assume all the marbles are the same size or do they imagine different size marbles in their jar?

4. I bought one pound of fruit. What might I have bought and how much might each piece weigh?

> Children will need various pieces of fruit to find their weights. Do they use a calculator to help them calculate how much of each type of fruit makes 1 pound? If not, how do they work this out?

5. A school bus has a 5,800-pound carrying capacity. How many people would it be permitted to carry?

> When working this out do children distinguish between adults and children? Discuss how bus companies work out how many people may travel on a bus. Do any children make allowances for baggage?

6. Sunni was carrying a small bucket that was full. When the bucket was put on the scales it weighed 1 pound exactly. What might be in the bucket?

> It is easy to think of objects that weigh 1 pound, but do they fill the bucket? Children may like to experiment with different items.

7. Make a list of some objects in your house that weigh between $\frac{1}{2}$ a pound and 1 pound.

> Allow the children to report on what they find. Is one weight more common than others?

Volume and Capacity (Grades K–2)

EXPERIENCES AT THIS LEVEL WILL HELP CHILDREN TO:
- use suitable language of comparison for volume and capacity
- fill containers by packing and pouring

- construct models with boxes or blocks
- choose and use nonstandard units of measure when comparing the size of two containers
- use nonstandard units to measure capacity
- compare two containers by pouring from one to the other
- estimate volume and capacity and improving estimates

MATERIALS
- boxes of various sizes and shapes
- assorted jars, cups, and other containers
- blocks or cubes
- rice, water, and so on

Good Questions and Teacher Notes

1. Find a container into which you can fit six cubes so that they do not move around too much.

> The container size will depend on the cube size. Are children aware that the cubes will fit certain shaped containers, such as rectangular prisms, better than a cylinder or a triangular prism?

2. How many containers can you find that will hold more than this jar?

> Note how children choose the containers. Are their estimates good? Do they pour from one container to another to check?

3. I filled a container with 20 spoonfuls of rice. What might the container that I used look like?

> Do children look for a range of containers and do their estimates improve as they continue to look?

4. Ella used twelve blocks to build a building. What might her building look like?

> Again, children should be able to build a range of models. Make time for them to see each other's buildings.

5. Sandy filled a container using 3 cups of water. What container might she have filled?

> This depends on the cup that was used. It is important to let children pour water to fill various containers so they can find possible ones.

Good Questions for Math Teaching

Volume and Capacity (Grades 3–4)

EXPERIENCES AT THIS LEVEL WILL HELP CHILDREN TO:
- use uniform materials, for example, cubes, to measure and compare volume and capacity
- choose appropriate units to measure and describe capacity
- compare and order capacity in common standard units
- make estimates and describe them appropriately
- improve estimates of volume and capacity

MATERIALS
- matchboxes, other boxes of various sizes and shapes
- assorted jars, cups, and other containers
- small cubes
- assorted soft drink and juice containers
- water, rice, sand, and so on

Good Questions and Teacher Notes

1. Design some box-shaped buildings using exactly twenty-four cubes.

> Recording is important. Ask the children to share their recording strategy. Could someone else build their building from the description?

2. Show the class a cup and a jug with the capacity of one of them obviously greater than the other. Ask, "Can you find a container with a capacity between this cup and this jug?"

> When children have found some containers you could put them in order of capacity too.

3. I packed sixteen little raisin boxes into a box so that they fit snugly. What might the box look like?

> Ask the children to devise an efficient way of describing their boxes, so that they could easily describe other designs. Can they see any patterns?

4. Can you find some containers that have the same capacity but a different shape?

> Children can do this either by packing or pouring.

5. Make a mark that would show when these drink containers are half full.

> Provide a range of containers such as orange juice, cola bottles, and so on. Note the strategies the children use.

6. A cubic structure is made out of twenty-seven smaller cubes. Two of the smaller cubes are removed from the larger structure. What might the structure look like?

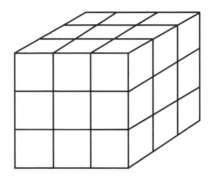

> It is important to allow children to use cubes to construct this rather than expecting them to visualize it.

7. A rectangular box is made out of cubes. The end of the box looks like this.

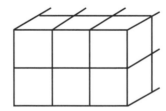

What might the volume of the box be?

> The answers are multiples of six. Let the children use cubes to do this.

8. At the supermarket Mom bought exactly 8 quarts of drink. She bought milk, some soft drinks, and some fruit juice. What might she have bought?

> You will need a range of drink containers for children to do this. This might be a suitable activity for children to do at home.

Volume and Capacity (Grades 5–6)

EXPERIENCES AT THIS LEVEL WILL HELP CHILDREN TO:

■ select suitable units and instruments to measure and compare capacity and volume
■ use smaller units for accuracy
■ read various measurements of capacity accurately
■ make and improve estimates of volume and capacity by comparing with known sizes of common objects

MATERIALS

■ assorted containers
■ cubes (interlocking and noninterlocking)
■ sand, water, and so on
■ light cardboard and paper to make models

Good Questions and Teacher Notes

1. I can see a container with a capacity bigger than 1 quart but smaller than 3 quarts. What might the container be?

> Some children may be able to do this by reading labels of containers (if attached).

2. Design some boxes that can hold thirty-six chocolates, each of which is a small cube.

> This could be a flat tray box with the cubes arranged as 6 x 6, 4 x 9, 3 x 12, 1 x 36 or 2 x 18. It could also have more than one layer. Are children aware of the possibilities?

3. Design a building constructed out of twenty cubes. It has some sections that are more than one story high. Draw your designs.

> The key feature of their designs is whether someone else can read the design and build it.

4. Two students measured the amount of water a container could hold. One wrote that it would hold 24 ounces. The other wrote that it would hold 22 ounces. How could this happen?

It is important for children to suggest a range of responses. Some possible responses are: one was holding the measuring container on an angle; one may have spilt some when pouring; the measuring container may have had some water in it already.

5. I made a shape from cubes. It looks like this diagram.

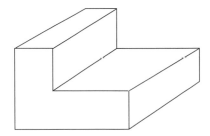

What might its volume be?

Can the students see a pattern? Can they find more than one possible answer? What answers are not possible?

6. A container holds 100 teaspoons of water. What might the container look like?

The children should share their strategies, especially for finding the volume of a teaspoon, with the class. Discuss the methods they use for recording their solutions.

7. A man says he will pay $1.00 for every grain of sand he can hold in his hand. How much might this be worth?

The children should share strategies. Some important variables are the size of the grains and the size of the hand.

8. I used some cubes to make a larger cube. How many cubes might I have used?

Do children understand what a cube is? Can they use a pattern when working this out, that is, 8 cubes will make a 2 x 2 x 2cm cube, 27 cubes will make a 3 x 3 x 3cm cube, 64 cubes will make a 4 x 4 x 4cm cube, and so on?

Area (Grades K–2)

EXPERIENCES AT THIS LEVEL WILL HELP CHILDREN TO:
■ describe surfaces by touching and looking

Good Questions for Math Teaching

- cover surfaces with a variety of flat objects
- estimate order of areas and check estimates by comparing directly or indirectly
- use appropriate language (For example, "This covers more than that.")

MATERIALS
- bottle tops
- 1-inch square tiles
- books

Good Questions and Teacher Notes

1. What are three things this page would completely cover?

> Children need to compare the page directly against other things. This question is to develop the idea of area as covering.

2. What are some things your hand will cover so that they cannot be seen? What are some things you cannot cover completely with your hand?

> This again develops the idea of area as covering and encourages children to compare areas by direct matching.

3. What are some things you could cover exactly with four books?

> This focuses more on covering a surface with repeat units, that is, books. Note if children choose books of the same size or different sizes, or if they use the same four books for each surface. Do they place the books close together so there are no gaps?

4. I covered an object with ten bottle tops. What might the object be?

> This encourages children to use repeating units to compare areas. Note if they are comfortable with placing the bottle tops in different arrangements or if they try to use the same arrangement to find objects. Do they put the bottle tops close together?

5. Max made a flat shape using five square tiles with their sides touching. What might Max's shape look like?

> The focus of this question is to show that different arrangements can have the same area. It is important for children to have enough tiles to make a variety of five-tile shapes.

Area (Grades 3–4)

EXPERIENCES AT THIS LEVEL WILL HELP CHILDREN TO:
- select suitable uniform units when comparing and measuring
- use accuracy, for example, leaving gaps affects the result
- use direct and indirect comparison to compare and order areas
- improve estimates of area

MATERIALS
- 1-inch square tiles
- various uniform units, for example, bottle tops or cards
- centimeter grids
- meter squares (make them out of newspaper joined with tape)

Good Questions and Teacher Notes

1. Using twelve square tiles, how many different rectangles can you make?

> The focus of this question is to show that different rectangular shapes can have the same area. It is a good idea to have children draw their rectangles showing the position of the tiles.

2. I am thinking of a shape with an area of thirty square tiles. What might the shape look like?

> If children cannot visualize this let them make some arrangements with thirty tiles to help them. They do not have to be rectangular.

3. I used twenty objects (all the same) to cover my table with no gaps. What might the objects be?

> Encourage children to guess before they do this. When they are trying objects note if they choose things that fit together without leaving gaps.

4. Sara covered approximately sixty-five squares on a centimeter grid. What object might she have used to cover the squares?

> This focuses on using uniform counting units to compare areas. Note how children handle parts of squares.

5. My grandmother bought a square rug and each side measured 2 yards. When she got it home it would not fit into the hallway so she cut the rug up and

joined the pieces together again to make a shape that would fit. What might her rug look like now?

> The focus of this question is to show that different shapes can have the same area.

6. Can you find some things that have a greater area than your desk top but not much greater? Can you find some things that have a smaller area than your desk top but not much smaller?

> This question is to make children use methods other than looking to compare areas. Note how they do this. Do they use uniform units to find surfaces just larger and just smaller?

7. It is possible to draw letters of the alphabet on grid paper. For example, this is what A would look like.

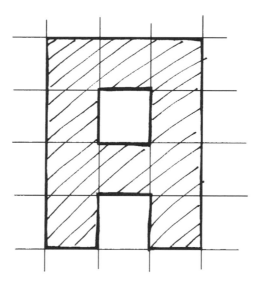

It takes ten squares. What other letters can be made in ten squares?

> The children need grid paper. They need to justify their answers.

8. A teddy bear left a footprint on grid paper. It measured eight squares. What might the footprint look like?

> The children need to discuss how they can count the squares when the shape does not completely cover a square.

9. A footprint was drawn on grid paper. Maggie said its area was twenty square units. Tony said that it was nineteen square units. How could this happen?

Measurement

The purpose of this question is to focus on the errors that can be made when calculating area by counting squares.

Area (Grades 5–6)

EXPERIENCES AT THIS LEVEL WILL HELP CHILDREN TO:

■ understand the importance of standard units
■ use conventional units
■ find or make different things with one measurement the same and another different, for example, same area/different perimeter
■ use known sizes of common things to help make estimates of area
■ describe the relationship among length, width, and area
■ measure and compare areas of rectangles in square units

MATERIALS

■ centimeter-squared paper; inch-squared paper
■ 1-inch square tiles

Good Questions and Teacher Notes

1. I want to make a vegetable garden in the shape of a rectangle. I have 200 feet of fence for my garden. What might the area of the garden be?

> This is to show that perimeter and area are different, and that shapes with the same perimeter may have different areas.

2. Draw some rectangles that have an area of 24cm².

> Note which children find all the possibilities by recording their answers methodically.

3. This letter *O* has an area of 6cm².

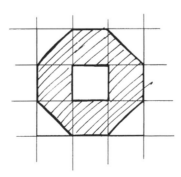

What letters can be drawn with an area of 6cm²?

> This is to emphasize that shapes of the same area can look different.

4. A rectangle has an area of 36cm². What might its perimeter be?

> Possible whole number side lengths and perimeters (in brackets) are 6 x 6 (24); 4 x 9 (26); 3 x 12 (30); 2 x 18 (40); 1 x 36 (74).

5. The area of a 4-by-4-foot-square table top is 16 square feet. By putting four tables together what shaped tables can I make and what is the perimeter of those shapes?

> Have square tiles for children to make different shapes of tables. The focus of this question is to show same area/different perimeters.

6. Sixty percent of a school property is building. One half of the rest is asphalt. What might the area of the property be, and what might the area of the asphalt be?

> This question combines fraction work with area. Note how realistic children's answers are.

7. Draw as many triangles as you can with an area of 6 square inches.

> You will find some children who are able to handle this question. It shows that there are many possibilities and that height and base are important, not the sides. Let children use squared paper. Using whole number multiples, the area can be achieved with base 1 and height 6 (1, 6), as well as (2, 3), (3, 2), and (6, 1).

8. The difference in areas of two rectangles is 32cm². What might the widths and lengths of the two rectangles be?

> Note how children start this one. The easiest way is to choose an area, say 100 square units, and then subtract 32 to find the other area. It is then just a matter of working out the widths and lengths of each rectangle.

Time (Grades K–2)

> EXPERIENCES AT THIS LEVEL WILL HELP CHILDREN TO:
> ■ use and respond to language that compares and describes time
> ■ order daily activities and sequence on a simple timeline

- learn names of days and months, and sequence months and seasons
- relate days and months to events in own life
- understand that clocks are used to tell the time and that analog and digital clocks provide the same information
- order times of day or of year by natural or cultural events
- know the function of a calendar and locate dates and events on it
- estimate time of day
- recognize o'clock and half-past times on an analog clock
- tell time on a digital clock in hours and minutes

MATERIALS
- calendars
- analog clock faces with movable hands
- a picture or photo of an event that happens during a school day
- a clock

Good Questions and Teacher Notes

1. What is something we could do that takes exactly one minute?

Rather than tell children what to use or do to measure a minute, it is interesting to see what they think is useful, and how they go about this. Their responses will tell you if they understand how long a minute actually is. If they say something like "count to sixty" or "walk down the hallway and back again," then you can be confident they have a good understanding. If they say something like "walk to the supermarket and back again" or "eat breakfast," then you can be reasonably sure their understanding is lacking.

2. What are some things you do in the morning and some things you do in the afternoon?

Children's responses will indicate if they know the distinction between these two time periods.

3. I know two people who have their birthday in the month before yours and two who have it in the month after yours. Who might they be?

Let children hear everyone's responses. This will help them to learn the sequence of months.

4. What is something you do in summer that you do not do in any other season?

This question will help children think about summer in a different way. They will relate it to something relevant to them. They can do this for the other seasons too.

5. Show the children a picture of something that happens during the day. Ask, "What are some things that happen before/after this picture?"

This focuses on the ordering of daily events into a sequence.

6. What things could you do that take about one hour?

This is similar to question #1 but does not require the exact measurement of one hour.

7. My mom said that I went to bed later than my usual bedtime of 8 o'clock. What time might I have gone to bed?

Note if children understand the concept of *later* as far as clock time goes.

8. What are some things you do each school day between 12 o'clock and 4 o'clock?

Are children able to relate daily events to clock time?

9. Show a time on an analog clock face with movable hands. Tell what you might be doing at that time on a school day.

See what children know about clock time.

Time (Grades 3–4)

EXPERIENCES AT THIS LEVEL WILL HELP CHILDREN TO:
- estimate time of day, week, or year using obvious indicators
- tell time on an analog clock
- measure with standard units using a variety of timers
- classify events according to duration of time
- calculate times before or after given times (minutes and hours)
- make and read simple schedules
- understand A.M. and P.M.
- knowing simple time facts, for example, sixty seconds = one minute, seven days = one week

MATERIALS
- analog clocks with seconds hands and digital clocks

- analog clock faces with movable hands
- calendars
- TV guides

Good Questions and Teacher Notes

1. There is something you do after you get out of bed and before you go to school that takes approximately four minutes. What might it be?

> Note if children can give reasonable suggestions.

2. In the summer, we are going on vacation for sixteen days. On what date might we leave on our vacation and on what date might we return?

> Discuss whether the children should count the day of departure and the day of return as part of the holiday. Do they use a pattern to work out the possibilities? Allow them to use a calendar if they want.

3. I left home and arrived at school forty-five minutes later. When might I have left home and when might I have arrived at school?

> Note if children are able to calculate times before or after a certain time.

4. The hands of a clock make an angle that is less than a quarter of a turn. What time might it be?

> Children who can work out an answer without using a clock face have strong visual ability. Let children use a clock face with movable hands if they want. Do children systematically record answers?

5. I am a month with thirty-one days. Which month might I be?

> Do children list all possibilities?

6. The hour hand is on the 7. The calendar says it is Tuesday. What might be on TV?

> Are children able to give all possible programs?

7. Richard took exactly thirty seconds to do each of three things. What might the three things have been?

> Children should be able to give reasonable suggestions to indicate that they know how long thirty seconds is.

8. I went on a vacation and made a snowman. What month of the year might it have been?

> The answers to this depend on where children go for their vacation. In New England, for example, it is likely to be in January or February, although this region gets snow at other times too.

9. What is something you can do about one hundred times in one minute?

> It is interesting to see how children work this out. Do they use the fact that sixty seconds = one minute and work in parts of a minute? Do they use trial and error?

10. Some workers started work exactly on the half hour and worked for six-and-a-quarter hours before stopping. When might they have started and when might they have stopped?

> This allows you to see if children are comfortable with calculating hours and minutes counting backward and forward. If the workers started at 6:30 they would finish at 12:45; at 7:30 they would finish at 1:45, and so on.

Time (Grades 5–6)

EXPERIENCES AT THIS LEVEL WILL HELP CHILDREN TO:
- estimate and measure time and duration of time
- use twelve-hour and twenty-four-hour timetables
- prepare feasible timetables and appreciate the importance of time in work situations
- move easily between digital and analog representations of time
- compare and use different calendars
- investigate various time zones

MATERIALS
- analog clocks with seconds hands and digital clocks
- maps of the local area
- TV guides

Good Questions and Teacher Notes

1. The time is now twenty minutes after 3 o'clock. Show this time in as many ways as you can.

> Children should be able to show analog and digital representations as well as use

numbers and words. While this may be easy for some, as an assessment tool this question will show what they all understand.

2. What are the times when the hour hand and the minute hand are at right angles?

Do children systematically record all the times this happens?

3. What is something you could do one thousand times in a day?

Are the children's responses possible? Encourage them to devise a method to test if their answers are possible. To do this they have to break the day into small parts.

4. A football game lasted two hours and fifteen minutes. What might be suitable starting and finishing times?

Note the methods used.

5. Our car trip took two and a half hours. We traveled at an average speed of 60 miles per hour. Describe our journey.

Let children use a map for this question. They might like to produce their own map to show the journey.

6. Sarah was allowed to watch television for a total of five hours from Monday through Friday. What might her TV schedule be for this week?

Can students read and interpret the TV schedule?

Length and Perimeter (Grades K–2)

EXPERIENCES AT THIS LEVEL WILL HELP CHILDREN TO:
- use and respond to appropriate language of comparison for length
- compare and order lengths by using direct and indirect measures
- measure using nonstandard units
- recognize the need for a common unit when direct comparison is not possible
- compare and estimate distances using everyday language
- be aware that perimeter is the length of a shape's boundary
- distinguish different length attributes, for example, length, width, height

Good Questions for Math Teaching

MATERIALS
- interlocking cubes
- lengths of card or paper, sticks, string
- 12-inch rulers

Good Questions and Teacher Notes

1. How many objects can you find that are longer than three handspans but shorter than four handspans?

> This question encourages children to use comparison language, for example, *almost as long as*, *exactly the same as*, and so on.

2. What is longer than two of your foot lengths but shorter than three of your foot lengths?

> Observe how children do questions #1 and #2. Do they line their handspans or foot lengths up against the object to be measured (direct)? Do they mark the length off on a card or piece of paper and then use this as their measurer (indirect)? Do they use a formal measuring instrument, like a ruler, to find how long three handspans or two foot lengths are and then use the ruler to measure other things? This last method is the most sophisticated. Children who use this should not be forced to use other methods unless they choose to.

3. Can you find something that is the same length as your height?

> Do children only measure vertical objects or do they understand that height is a length measurement? Discuss why things vary between children, for example, some are taller than others.

4. Give the children a stick or piece of string. Ask, "Can you find some things longer than/shorter than/the same length as your string?"

> This question establishes if children understand the concepts of longer/shorter/same length as.

5. What is there in this room that is three handspans long?

> This question encourages children to use length vocabulary when talking about their findings, for example, *much longer*, *almost as long as*, *exactly the same as*, and so on.

6. This string is a measure of the distance around an object in this room. What is the object?

This question can be used to introduce the concept of perimeter.

7. There are five children standing together. If you are the middle person in height, who might the other four be?

This activity requires children to compare and order heights. Note how they do this, for example, directly or by using an instrument.

8. Tara measured a table and said that it was ten sticks long. Michael measured the same table and said it was twelve sticks long. How might this happen?

Some possible reasons are: the two sets of sticks they used were different; Tara did not put her sticks exactly end to end; Michael did not measure in a straight line; Tara did not start at the edge of the table; the sticks used by either child varied in length.

9. What are some things that are about 1 foot long?

Give children a 12-inch ruler to use. This activity gives children experience comparing objects to the standard measure of 1 foot.

10. Guess how many cubes long an object is. Then snap together cubes to check. Repeat for other objects.

See if children's guesses improve as they measure different objects.

Length and Perimeter (Grades 3–4)

EXPERIENCES AT THIS LEVEL WILL HELP CHILDREN TO:
- realize the need for standard units
- select a suitable unit to measure and compare lengths and perimeters
- realize the importance of accuracy
- measure and record length
- improve estimates of length and perimeter

MATERIALS
- rulers, both customary and metric
- string
- Cuisenaire rods

Good Questions and Teacher Notes

1. What could we use a yard stick or meter stick to measure?

> Children should choose suitable objects to measure. They should measure horizontal and vertical lengths.

2. What in this room is longer than 1 foot but less than 2 feet?

> Children should be able to estimate things between 1 foot and 2 feet in length.

3. Can you find something that is about twice as long as it is high? What is the length of each?

> Note if everyone understands the language used, for example, *long, high*. Check how confident children are with doubling and halving.

4. Give children a piece of string. Say, "This string is the distance around some objects. What might some of those objects be?"

> Watch what children choose to compare the string against. Are they choosing objects that have a perimeter about the same length as their string? Do their choices improve with practice?

5. What can you find that has a perimeter of 30cm?

> Do children understand the concept of perimeter? Are they looking at the measurement around shapes? Do they use a suitable strategy to measure perimeter?

6. How many things can you find that are 1 inch long? One foot long?

> Note if children choose suitable objects to measure and if they use a ruler correctly.

7. How many things can you find that are 1cm long? 10cm long?

> Give children each a white and orange Cuisenaire rod to use, or a metric ruler.

8. Can you find anyone with the same foot length as yours? With the same foot perimeter?

> Notice how children solve the problem of measuring their foot perimeter. You may suggest that they trace their foot on paper.

Measurement

Length and Perimeter (Grades 5–6)

EXPERIENCES AT THIS LEVEL WILL HELP CHILDREN TO:

- recognize that a smaller unit will give a more accurate measurement
- select appropriate measuring instruments
- read measurement marks accurately
- devise and use own methods to find the perimeter of polygons
- use known lengths to help and improve estimates
- find or make different things with one measurement the same and another different, for example, same area/different perimeter

MATERIALS

- rulers, both customary and metric
- string
- centimeter-squared paper
- inch-squared paper

Good Questions and Teacher Notes

1. How many differently-shaped rectangles can you make with a piece of string 3 feet long? What are their areas?

> Children will find it easier to work with others to do this so they can hold the corners. Some of them may not need to use the string. Note if they record their answers methodically.

2. What might the length of a garden fence be if the area of the garden is 12 square yards?

> Children can learn that even though the area is fixed, the perimeter can vary. It helps them to better understand the concepts of perimeter and area. Possible whole number lengths are 3 x 4, 6 x 2, 12 x 1.

3. I have drawn a shape on centimeter-squared paper with a perimeter of 16cm. What might my shape look like?

> Give children centimeter-squared paper to use. Tell them that shapes do not have to be rectangles, but they should draw on the grid lines. Have them compare the areas of the shapes they draw.

Good Questions for Math Teaching

4. Measure the area of a book cover with centimeter-squared paper and inch-squared paper. Compare the measurements and write about the relationship between square centimeters and square inches.

> Students should become bilingual in measurement—able to use both systems.

5. Draw different shapes with the same area. Compare their perimeters.

> Children can use either inches or centimeters.

6 Space

The three topics included in this strand are:

1. location and position
2. two-dimensional shapes
3. three-dimensional shapes

Because we use spatial knowledge for a wide range of practical tasks, such as finding our way around, designing, and so on, it follows that many of the experiences in this strand can be done in a practical manner using concrete materials.

Children can be encouraged to handle and make things using a variety of materials, to produce models, and to change the size, shape, and position of objects. They should be given many opportunities to talk about their work. Their spatial language will develop as they describe their own experiences and listen to others describe theirs.

In the upper grades children need experiences that allow them to look more closely at the properties of shape and design and thus refine their thinking and descriptions.

The children's experiences when working on these questions will assist them to develop their spatial concepts and allow you to build up an accurate picture of each child's knowledge.

Location and Position (Grades K–2)

EXPERIENCES AT THIS LEVEL WILL HELP CHILDREN TO:

■ use and understand language of relative positions in space, such as *under, behind, up, between,* and so on
■ follow directions and give oral directions
■ find and name locations with relationships such as *near to*
■ find and name locations on simple maps

MATERIALS

■ outdoor playground equipment

Good Questions and Teacher Notes

1. What are some things in this room that you can go under?

   Note if children do go *under* objects.

2. Allow children to walk around the room until you say "Stop." Then ask, "Who has the door behind them?," "Who is near the door?," and so on.

   This will show you which children understand the meaning of certain location or position words. Make up questions for the words and concepts you want to check.

3. I took two steps and finished near the desk. Where might I have started?

   There are various possible responses for this activity. Do any children insist there is only one? Note how they work this out. One good way is to work backward from the desk.

4. Make your own obstacle course by going over three things, through one thing, under one thing, and between two things.

   Adapt this to check the concepts you want. This is a good activity to do outside on the playground equipment.

5. Where could you stand in this room so the door is to your left/right?

   This will let you see if children know left and right. Do it for other objects in the room too.

Good Questions for Math Teaching

6. What can you see that is in front of the teacher's desk?

> Again, this tests if children understand the concept of *in front of*. Use the same idea to check other words.

7. If I walk out of our room and turn right where might I be heading?

> Children should be able to give a range of responses, not just the first thing they would come to.

8. I can see something above the book shelves and below the blinds. What could it be?

> Adapt this to suit your situation. You could turn it into an *I Spy* game. The purpose is to assess if children understand the meaning of location language.

Location and Position (Grades 3–4)

EXPERIENCES AT THIS LEVEL WILL HELP CHILDREN TO:
- make maps of familiar places and read maps from street directories, atlases, and so on
- be aware of the order and proximity of objects on maps
- use and respond to the correct language to describe maps and locations, for example, *north, right angle*
- describe and visualize simple movement sequences

MATERIALS
- street directories
- atlases
- grid paper

Good Questions and Teacher Notes

1. I walked from one place to another. I took three steps forward, turned left, took another three steps forward, and turned left again. Where might I have started and where would I finish?

> This is to help children visualize a sequence of movements. Their answer depends on where they started from.

2. Paula took ten steps to the north, turned right and walked east for twenty steps. Where might she have started her journey and where might she have finished?

Again, this encourages children to visualize movements. It also lets you observe if they understand some directional language.

3. What are some things that are south of where you are now?

Note if children understand that south is not just their immediate environment. Do any of them use a map to locate towns or cities that are to the south?

4. Ask your parents to help you draw a plan or map of the outside walls of your house. Draw in the rooms by yourself.

You could let children do this activity on grid paper. Make sure that they get an opportunity to see other sketches and talk about the different plans. They could also discuss their plans with their parents.

5. When Mrs. Smith leaves her home she travels in a westerly direction to get to work. What suburb might she live in?

This depends on where work is. Note how children go about this one. Have street directories available for them to look at.

Location and Position (Grades 5–6)

EXPERIENCES AT THIS LEVEL WILL HELP CHILDREN TO:
- use distance, direction, compass points, coordinates, and angles (multiples of 45°) to read and give instructions
- draw maps and plans to various specifications
- use maps to plan a trip
- make and read maps using simple scale ideas, for example, 1 inch = 1 mile

MATERIALS
- a world map and a map of the United States of America
- a road map of your area
- rulers (for using a scale)
- grid paper

Good Questions and Teacher Notes

1. Pedro went on a vacation to a place near the equator. Where might he have gone?

Some children do not understand what the equator is and think that there can only be one answer for this.

Good Questions for Math Teaching

2. Someone asks you to give them directions to reach a large town near your home. What directions would you give?

> This depends on where you start. Can children give a variety of responses? Can other children interpret their directions accurately?

3. Friends of ours gave their vacation destination as north of St. Louis, Missouri, and west of New York City. Where might they be going?

> Like question #1, children will see that there is more than one possibility. Note if they use coordinates correctly.

4. Name some places east/north/south/west of your town or city.

> Check that children are confident with directions.

5. Design a maze.

> You may like to discuss the characteristics of a maze first. The children could try to solve each other's mazes.

6. Redesign this classroom using the same furniture as we have already. Present your design on a map or plan drawn to scale.

> Children may like to use grid paper. Have them explain their designs to the class. It is important that the designs are functional.

7. I want to go on a long bike trip. I want to ride at least 500 miles but not more than 750 miles. Where might I travel?

> The children need to use a detailed map with a scale rather than one with distances marked on it. They should justify their answers. They might like to discuss how they measured the distance along curved roads.

Two-Dimensional Shapes (Grades K–2)

EXPERIENCES AT THIS LEVEL WILL HELP CHILDREN TO:
- make and draw reasonable representations of common shapes, for example, triangles
- recognize and name common shapes
- match two-dimensional figures to faces of three-dimensional shapes
- use appropriate language to talk about shapes, for example, *round, corner, side,* and so on

Space

- make pictures and patterns with shapes
- recognize symmetry and make symmetrical pictures

MATERIALS

- pattern blocks

Good Questions and Teacher Notes

1. What is it that makes these shapes triangles?

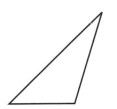 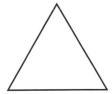 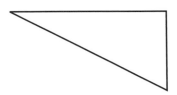

This makes children think about the properties of triangles rather than just draw any shape with three sides. It allows you to see if they are aware of any other properties of triangles other than three sides.

2. I drew a shape with four sides. Draw what my shape might look like.

It is a good idea to have a shape drawn (but hidden) so children can compare their shapes with it. It is important that children see all the four-sided shapes that are produced.

3. Peter said that he used two smaller shapes both the same to cover his large shape. If his large shape looked like this what might the two smaller shapes look like?

Give children paper rectangles, all the same as the sample, so they can experiment cutting it into two pieces in different ways.

4. A friend of mine sorted these shapes into two groups. What might the two groups have been?

Good Questions for Math Teaching

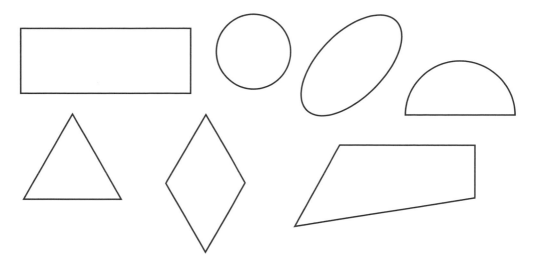

This allows children to group shapes according to properties. For example, they could choose regular/irregular shapes, curved/linear shapes, 4-sides/others, and so on. Ask them to tell you why they have chosen the groups; do not assume you know their reasoning.

5. I made a picture using only circles and squares. What might my picture have looked like?

Check if children do only use circles and squares. Display finished pictures.

6. Make a design with pattern blocks. What did you make?

Children will explore how shapes can fit together.

Two-Dimensional Shapes (Grades 3–4)

EXPERIENCES AT THIS LEVEL WILL HELP CHILDREN TO:
- use suitable spatial language to describe and compare shapes
- copy and make patterns that involve translations, reflections, and rotations
- explore transformations of shapes
- decide if shapes will or will not tessellate
- develop ideas of angle as an amount of turn
- identify, construct, and order, angles using direct comparison and appropriate instruments

■ construct two-dimensional shapes with a variety of materials
■ recognize and draw straight, curved, and parallel lines

MATERIALS
■ pattern blocks
■ a clock face with moveable hands
■ geoboards and rubber bands

Good Questions and Teacher Notes

1. Write down everything you know and everything you can find out about this square.

The main purpose of this question is for the children to become aware of what they know. They should also see that even in simple figures there are many mathematical concepts. Their responses can include comments on: equal sides; equal angles; actual measurements of sides; the perimeter; the area; the lengths of the diagonals; the symmetry, and so on.

2. On a page draw five lines, no two of which are parallel.

Ask children to check each other's drawings to see if they agree.

3. I am thinking of a shape. It tessellates, which means many of them fit together like tiles, with no spaces. What might the shape be?

If you have lots of small shapes children could check their own answers by seeing if they fit together. Some of them may need to use these shapes to answer the question. Some shapes that tessellate are triangles, squares, rectangles, hexagons, and some irregular shapes.

4. Using four triangles from the pattern blocks, how many different shapes can you make? Draw them.

Ask children to devise a way to check if their shapes are the same or different. (If you do not have access to pattern blocks, cut out four same-size triangles for each student.)

5. A lot of things in our room have angles that are the same as a quarter turn.

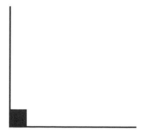

What can you see like this?

> Let children use the corner of a sheet of paper.

6. I was watching television and I noticed that the hands of a clock made an acute angle. What program might I have been watching?

> Children might like to use a clock to do this. As they are working, check that they know what an acute angle is.

7. I drew a shape with four sides but none of the four sides were the same length. Draw what my shape might have looked like.

> This activity is similar to question #2 (see Grades K–2), but it excludes squares and rectangles by stating that no sides were the same length.

8. Bart made five squares on his geoboard, all of which were different sizes. What might Bart's geoboard have looked like?

> Children should work with a partner and share a geoboard. As they complete the five squares they should draw them on paper before beginning a new set of squares. Allow time for pairs to share their geoboard patterns with others.

Two-Dimensional Shapes (Grades 5–6)

EXPERIENCES AT THIS LEVEL WILL HELP CHILDREN TO:

- use perspective to represent three-dimensional shapes as two-dimensional
- give clear descriptions of shapes
- produce complex symmetrical patterns
- construct tessellations and explain why shapes will or will not tessellate

- enlarge and reduce two-dimensional figures
- identify and classify angles
- construct common shapes
- identify and describe horizontal, vertical, and diagonal lines

MATERIALS
- measuring equipment
- protractors
- a clock with moveable hands
- small mirrors
- drawing paper

Good Questions and Teacher Notes

1. If I took two steps forward, turned right 60 degrees, took another two steps forward and turned right 60 degrees, and kept doing this, this is the path I would walk.

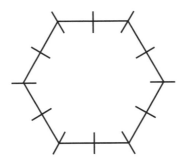

What are the instructions for some other shapes?

> Let children check each other's work by following the instructions and seeing if they make the shape they say it does.

2. The fourth-grade children said they were going to mark out a basketball court. Write down the instructions they need to follow.

> You would expect the children to describe the length of the lines, the angles, the size of the circles, and so on, so that a fourth-grade child could understand. Let them check each other's instructions by actually marking out a court.

3. I cut out a shape, folded it in half, and showed the new folded shape to my teacher. She said it had a line of symmetry. What might my original shape have looked like?

Good Questions for Math Teaching

Allow children to make some shapes and fold them. Can they explain symmetry? You could display the finished shapes.

4. Tan told me he drew a shape that had no diagonals. What might his shape look like?

Do the children realize that their shapes must be curved?

5. If I drew a shape and the total of the angles in the shape was 180 degrees what could the shape be?

Children can draw any triangle they like. They may like to use a protractor to check the size of the angles.

6. I wrote a capital letter so that it had rotational symmetry. What might the letter have been?

Rotational symmetry means you can turn the letter and it still looks the same, for example, *S* and *H*.

7. A shape has at least two sides 2 inches long and at least two sides 4 inches long. One angle is 90 degrees, one angle is less, but the rest are more. What might the shape look like?

After children have completed some shapes, let them check in pairs that their shapes follow the instructions.

8. A shape is made of two smaller shapes that are the same shape and the same size and that are not rectangles. What might the larger shape look like?

Check if children have followed directions. Can anyone work out how to check that the smaller shapes are congruent?

9. My friend was sure that she had made a rectangle. The teacher said it was not a rectangle. How can my friend check if it is a rectangle?

Children should be looking at the size of the angles as well as the length of the lines. Would the definition that children produce allow a square to be a rectangle?

10. Suzy drew a box while I watched. I then drew one in a different way. How might I have drawn it?

Children should have the opportunity to see a variety of styles of representing three-dimensional shapes drawn in two dimensions.

Space

Three-Dimensional Shapes (Grades K–2)

EXPERIENCES AT THIS LEVEL WILL HELP CHILDREN TO:

■ build from imagination, memory, visual instruction, or oral description
■ choose pieces that meet functional requirements
■ copy simple arrangements of shapes
■ identify and name common three-dimensional shapes in the environment
■ use and understand functional spatial language, for example, *stacks, rolls*
■ use simple language to describe objects
■ classify shapes according to function and attributes
■ distinguish between a three-dimensional object and its faces
■ investigate the shape of cross sections of three-dimensional objects

MATERIALS

■ lots of three-dimensional objects, for example, cylinders, boxes, cones
■ a cardboard box
■ blocks and other stacking shapes

Good Questions and Teacher Notes

1. In my hand I have an object that is able to roll. What might it be?

Children should realize that a ball is not the only object that will roll. You could provide a variety of objects for them to try.

2. What objects in this room could pass through this opening?

Make a rectangular opening about 2 inches by 8 inches by cutting into a cardboard box. Note how well children visualize before selecting an object to try.

3. I can see a box-shaped object in this room. What object can I see?

Use whatever shape you want for this question. It allows you to see any misconceptions children have about the attributes of a particular shape. For example, some children may think a box shape is only a cube.

4. We stacked some objects to make a wall. What objects might we have used?

As children are working, note the attributes of the shapes they choose. Do they try to stack shapes with curved surfaces?

5. In a bag I can feel that an object has flat faces, sharp corners, and straight edges. What might this object be?

Do children understand the spatial terms that are used?

6. I traced around one of the faces of an object. The shape I drew was a circle. What might the object have been?

The focus of this question is to help children distinguish between a three-dimensional object and its faces.

7. Sara used three rolling shapes, four boxes, and one cone to build something. What did she build and what might her construction look like?

Let children use suitable three-dimensional objects to construct this. Look at the variety of responses.

8. From the top a stack of blocks looks like this diagram:

Use a set of blocks to show what the stack might look like.

Most children will make a stack with a flat top. Point out that the top does not have to be flat and then let children explore this further.

Three-Dimensional Shapes (Grades 3–4)

EXPERIENCES AT THIS LEVEL WILL HELP CHILDREN TO:
- recognize three-dimensional shapes from drawings or photos taken from various perspectives
- identify and draw different cross sections of three-dimensional shapes
- make common solids from clay
- draw and make nets of common solids, and matching shapes with nets

- use increasingly accurate language to describe objects
- classify and compare solids according to their features and properties
- explore repetitions of objects in structures

MATERIALS
- photographs of aerial views
- various containers and packaging from foodstuffs
- fruit and vegetables
- blocks

Good Questions and Teacher Notes

1. What do you know and what can you find out about a pyramid?

> The main purpose of this question is for the children to become aware of what they know. They should realize that even in common figures there are many mathematical concepts. Their responses can include comments on: the number of sides; the number of faces; the shape of the base; whether they can be stacked, and so on.

2. When I looked at a photograph taken from an airplane I saw rectangular and circular shapes. What might these shapes be?

> It is sometimes difficult for children to visualize this, although those who have been in an airplane should have a good idea. If possible show them some aerial views to help them. You could also build a city or something similar with blocks and let children view it from above.

3. At the supermarket Mom bought a container shaped like a rectangular prism but the label came off. What might have been in the container?

> This might be a question that children can do at home or when they next visit a supermarket. Keep a class list of suitable items. It can be added to as children find containers.

4. When I cut some fruit and vegetables into two pieces the cross section (or inside surface) looked like this:

What fruit and vegetables might I have cut?

> It is a good idea to have some fruit and vegetables available for children to cut to find which ones can be cut like the diagram.

5. These shapes were sorted into two groups. What might the groups be?

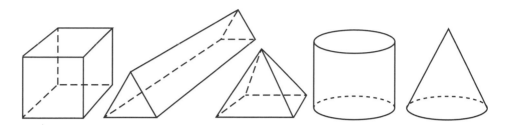

> It is likely that there will be a wide range of responses. It is important to ask the children to justify their answers.

6. Jack and David built a building using thirty bricks. What might their building look like?

> Children must use the blocks to construct one building, not a group of buildings. Make sure they have time to see the variety of possible responses.

7. From the top a stack of blocks looks like this:

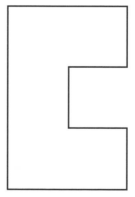

What might it look like from the front?

> This activity is similar to question #8 (see Grades K–2). Again, some children will not realize that the top does not have to be flat, and this will affect their view of the front. Likewise, the front does not have to be even.

8. We went on a walk. The plan was for everyone to write down the names of objects we saw and the name of the shape of that object. I wrote down the names of some of the shapes we saw but I forgot to write the name of the object next to its shape name. Can you help me work out what they might have been?

cylinder	
triangular pyramid	
cone	
rectangular prism	
sphere	

This question will identify if children know the characteristics of these shapes. Can they identify more than one object for each shape? Give them time to share their findings.

Three-Dimensional Shapes (Grades 5–6)

EXPERIENCES AT THIS LEVEL WILL HELP CHILDREN TO:

- represent three-dimensional shapes on a two-dimensional surface and select objects to match three-dimensional representations
- make complex models, including those that use combinations of three-dimensional objects
- use accurate language to describe objects
- compare objects using all aspects of their features and properties
- investigate translations, rotations, and reflections in objects and formations
- enlarge simple three-dimensional objects

MATERIALS

- plastic straws and joiners or clay
- overhead projector
- squares made from light cardstock and squared paper
- cubes

Good Questions and Teacher Notes

1. I have twelve plastic straws and eight joiners. What model's skeleton can I make?

> Have straws and joiners available for children to use. You may use clay to join straws. Display the finished models and discuss their diversity.

2. My friend was making a container and had cut out all the surfaces. He asked me if I would put it together for him. Altogether there were eight surfaces. What might his finished container look like?

> This is quite difficult to visualize. It will be easier for children to find some containers that have eight surfaces. You could keep an area aside for displaying them.

3. Six squares were joined together with one whole side of each touching at least one whole side of another square, but they could not be folded to make a box. What might the arrangement of squares look like?

> As well as allowing children to join six squares together to try to make a box, also allow them to cut up boxes in different ways so that the six surfaces join. Another approach might be to give the children squared paper and have them draw the sets of six squares, then cut them out to check whether they can be folded into a box. Display finished sets of squares.

4. From the top a stack of blocks looks like this:

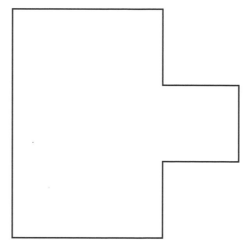

Draw what the stack might look like.

A similar question to this appears in each of the other sections of three-dimensional shape. This question varies in that it emphasizes drawing the shape rather than making it. Children can still make the shape with blocks. Note that even though the cross section looks flat, the faces of the shape do not have to be.

5. A stack of cubes was made, glued together, and then painted on the outside. Eight of the cubes were painted on exactly two sides. What might the stack look like?

> The shape does not have to be regular. The children may have to discuss what *exactly two sides* means.

7 Chance and Data

The two topics included in this strand are:

1. chance
2. data

As many situations involve chance, it is important that we provide activities that will develop children's understanding of chance and allow them to handle chance situations confidently. The experiences provided by these questions range from allowing children to make predictions about the likelihood of an event occurring to developing their ability to identify and record all outcomes in a systematic manner.

The data topic provides children with opportunities to collect, organize, represent, and interpret data from situations that are both relevant and of interest to them. They are also encouraged to determine the appropriateness and quality of data collection and presentation so that they may develop a discerning approach to interpreting data.

Children's confidence and competence in working with chance and data will be developed by working on these questions.

Chance (Grades K–2)

EXPERIENCES AT THIS LEVEL WILL HELP CHILDREN TO:

■ recognize that some events involve chance
■ use and understand chance expressions
■ recognize that different results are possible when the same event is repeated
■ classify events as certain, possible, or impossible
■ compare possible events
■ distinguish *impossible* from *unlikely*
■ predicting results and comparing with the outcome

MATERIALS

■ coins
■ dice

Good Questions and Teacher Notes

1. If two coins are tossed, what could happen?

> It is important that children actually toss two coins many times so that they can observe what happens. The main point is for them to see that there are three different outcomes for the one event and that any of the three can happen. Some of them may realize that the heads/tails combination occurs more often and start to think about why this is.

2. I overheard my mother telling our neighbor that on the weekend we would definitely do something but I couldn't hear what it was. What might it be?

> Children's responses will indicate if they understand the meaning of *definitely*. What is definite for some will not be so for others, so it is good for them to hear what others think and recognize this.

3. I heard the teacher say, "It is . . . that all of the children in this class will watch television tonight" but I didn't hear one of the words. What might the missing word be? What is something that is more likely to happen than what the teacher is talking about?

> The children may need to discuss what the question is asking them to do. Ask them to explain it in their own words. Perhaps some of them could discuss how often they watch television.

4. Two children were playing a dice game. One child tossed two dice together and when they landed one was a 6 and one was a 4. What other number combinations might the child have tossed?

> Note whether children give a range of responses.

5. Someone asked the teacher a question and she replied "Maybe." What might the question be?

> This is similar to question #2 and the way children interpret *maybe* depends on previous experiences with the word. It is worth discussing what *maybe* means to different children, or what it means when certain people say it—for example, if Mom says it, it might mean *No*, whereas if Dad says it, it generally means *Yes*.

6. Sophie put her in-line skates on for the first time, stood up and. . . . What might have happened next?

> This question focuses on the range of outcomes that are possible. Can the children list all of the possible outcomes?

7. When we were playing a dice game where we had to throw a 6 on one of the dice to start, Emma said, "Let's make it that we have to throw a 3 instead of a 6 because it is easier." Do you agree with her? Why?

> This will allow you to see if children have any misconceptions about the chances involved in tossing a dice.

8. A family has three children. We know that at least one of the children is a girl. Draw what the family might look like.

> Can children give all possibilities?

9. Child: "Can I go out with my friend in one hour?"
   Mom: "It is possible it will be dark then."
What might the time be now?

> The children's responses will depend on the month and daylight saving. Discuss whether they know when it will get dark today.

10. Our class wrote down some things that we felt were *impossible*. What might we have written?

> You can use a similar question for *certain* too. It is important to discuss what different children have written.

Chance (Grades 3–4)

EXPERIENCES AT THIS LEVEL WILL HELP CHILDREN TO:

- identify and record all possible outcomes from simple chance experiments
- identify some outcomes as being equally likely
- use simple techniques for random selection
- order events from *most likely* to *least likely* and justify choice
- realize how an outcome can be influenced
- appreciate the idea of fair and unfair in simple games

MATERIALS

- dice
- a bag and tiles, at least two colors

Good Questions and Teacher Notes

1. Madeleine threw two dice and when they landed she subtracted one number from the other and wrote down the answer 1. What might the numbers on each have been?

> Can children give all possible outcomes? Allow them to use dice if they wish.

2. In a bag there are some tiles. I draw out one tile and it is red. I put it back and draw again. This time the tile is blue. I put it back. After ten draws, I have drawn out three red and seven blue. How many tiles might there be in the bag and how many might be blue?

> There might be any number of tiles in the bag, but we suspect that they are mainly red and blue. The proportions do not have to be 3 to 7, but it is likely that there are more blue than red. The children might like to do some experiments.

3. My brother was complaining that it always rained on his birthday and spoiled the activities that had been planned. When might his birthday be?

> It is important that children justify their choice of time here.

4. My older sister was talking to Dad and asked him a question. His reply was, "It is more likely than unlikely." What might the question be?

> Children should be asked to justify their question. This activity focuses on the language of chance.

Good Questions for Math Teaching

5. Design a board game where it is easier for you to win than your opponent.

> It is important that children test their games out by playing against each other. Which games are obviously "rigged" and which are more subtly "rigged"?

Chance (Grades 5–6)

EXPERIENCES AT THIS LEVEL WILL HELP CHILDREN TO:
- analyze outcomes from simple chance experiments
- use appropriate language of chance
- use a numerical scale for chance events
- interpret probability statements
- design a simple random device to produce a specified order of probability

MATERIALS
- a bag and tiles (at least two colors)
- materials to make board games
- playing cards
- cubes to make dice
- materials to make spinners
- blank cards to write numbers on

Good Questions and Teacher Notes

1. I chose five tiles from a bag of tiles without looking. I noticed that there were three red and two blue. What might the color of the tiles in the bag be and how many tiles might there be?

> This is similar to question #2 (see Grades 3–4). There is a range of possible answers, but the three red and two blue outcome should be reasonable given the breakdown of the tiles in the bag. In other words, if the children suggest there are one hundred tiles, the number of each color should be close to sixty red and forty blue. Of course other colors are possible as well.

2. The probability of an event is $\frac{1}{3}$. What might the event be?

> Can children offer a range of suitable responses? You may have to discuss what $\frac{1}{3}$ means. Children should justify their responses.

3. What words could be used to describe an event with a probability of 0.6?

> Again, this checks if children can interpret numerical statements of probability. Some possible words are *good chance*, and *better than even chance*.

Chance and Data

4. A new family was moving into the house next door to us. We had been told that there were five children but we did not know if they were girls or boys. I hoped they were girls and my brother hoped they were boys. What might the genders of the children in the family be?

> Are children able to list all possibilities? As they are doing this note those who do it systematically.

5. I heard the radio announcer say that something had an "even chance." What might he have been talking about?

> Do children's answers reflect an understanding of "even chance"?

6. A toy manufacturer wants to design a die where the chance of throwing a "red" is $\frac{1}{2}$. What might the die look like?

> As long as half of the faces are red, it does not matter what the others are. Children could make their dice and test them out.

7. Using a small deck of cards you have a $\frac{1}{4}$ chance of choosing a picture card and a $\frac{1}{2}$ chance of drawing an even number. What might the cards in the deck be?

> It is a good idea to let children experiment with some playing cards to help them do this one.

8. We spun a spinner lots of times. It landed on blue most of the time, on red some of the time, and only once on white and yellow. Draw what the spinner face might look like.

> You could make spinners, let the children color them in how they think and then try them to see what results.

9. There were four cards in a container. One card had the number 2 on it, another had 5, another had 4, and the last had 7. I had to select two of the cards at a time. On my first try I selected 5 and 7. What other combinations might I have selected?

> Do children record the combinations systematically? Do they record all possible combinations?

10. I tested something one hundred times. I got the result I wanted for seventy of the times, but not the other thirty. What might I have been doing?

> Accept all reasonable suggestions. Make sure that the children can justify their suggestions.

Good Questions for Math Teaching

Data (Grades K–2)

EXPERIENCES AT THIS LEVEL WILL HELP CHILDREN TO:

- decide what data to collect and how to collect it to answer questions
- represent data concretely and pictorially
- compare information by counting
- sort and sequence data
- make simple pictographs and block graphs using one-to-one correspondence
- describe results from data collection and display
- interpret visual representations

MATERIALS

- materials to make graphs, for example, blocks, beads and string, and so on

Good Questions and Teacher Notes

1. What might this be the graph of?

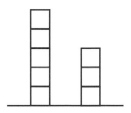

Do children make reasonable suggestions? Are some suggestions more plausible than others?

2. You did a survey to find out who was happy and who was sad. What pictures could you use to represent these feelings?

Make a display of their suggestions.

3. The twenty-five children in our class each drew a picture of him- or herself. Our teacher asked a question that we could answer with a "yes" or a "no." Twenty children put their picture in the *yes* column while five children put their picture in the *no* column. What might the question have been?

Are the suggestions made by children reasonable? Make a class chart of possible questions.

4. How could you make a representation of the children in our class who can swim and the children who cannot?

> It is important that children have the opportunity to see the variety of representations used.

5. On a graph about pets owned by children in our class, I counted more dogs than cats. What might the graph look like?

> Children can represent this how they want. Do they realize that the graph may show other pets as well? Allow time for them to explain their graphs to others.

Data (Grades 3–4)

> EXPERIENCES AT THIS LEVEL WILL HELP CHILDREN TO:
> - collect data to answer questions
> - plan appropriate and efficient ways to organize data
> - improve descriptions of categories
> - use many-to-one correspondence to display data
> - represent data on bar graphs
> - interpret information from tables and graphs
>
> MATERIALS
> - materials to make graphs, for example, blocks, beads and string, and so on

Good Questions and Teacher Notes

1. I did a survey of my third-grade class. This is what the graph looks like.

```
X
X
X  X
X  X  X
X  X  X  X
X  X  X  X  X
─────────────────
1  2  3  4  5
```

What might the survey be about?

Are children's suggestions reasonable? Discuss why some suggestions are more plausible than others. The class might like to do a survey to check whether some of the suggestions are possible or reasonable.

2. This is a graph about a fourth-grade class. What is it about? How many children might there be in the class?

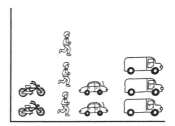

The main point here is that each symbol might represent more than one child. Do children realize this and do they give reasonable responses?

3. This graph shows the proportion of children in a class who prefer particular shows.

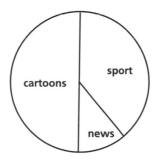

How many children might be in the class and how many prefer each show? Present the data a different way.

Note how children approach this. Do they decide how many children are in the class first or do they try to work out how many children would be in each category first? Do they realize that there must be an even number of children in the class? Allow time to share their presentations and discuss the most effective ways to present the data.

Chance and Data

4. This is a graph of how hungry you are.

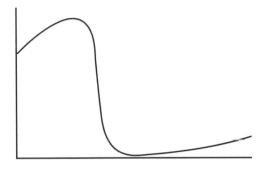

What times of day might be represented by the graph?

> Can children relate points on the graph to appropriate times of day? They might like to discuss what the graph would look like near meal times, and before and after meal times.

5. These are the results of a survey.

Place	Tally
library	///
playground	++++ ++++ //
under the trees	++++ //
driveway	///

What might the survey be about?

> Accept any reasonable suggestions. For example, it could be a survey of where children like playing, a survey to show where accidents have happened, and so on.

6. A graph showed that among a class of children the most popular footwear was sneakers. The next most popular was boots. The next was sandals and the least popular was thongs. What might the graph look like?

> This question allows children to interpret the data in their own way. Look for those who display data using many-to-one correspondence. Display finished graphs.

7. In a survey of this class exactly half the children said "yes" and half said "no." What might the survey be about?

Good Questions for Math Teaching

Are children's responses reasonable? You might like to do a survey with the class to check whether the suggestions are reasonable.

Data (Grades 5–6)

EXPERIENCES AT THIS LEVEL WILL HELP CHILDREN TO:

- suggest what data to collect to answer questions
- prepare questionnaires where necessary to collect data
- record data systematically
- construct bar graphs and use scales on axes
- represent and interpret data on a wide range of graphs, tables, and diagrams
- use a database to enter and extract information
- use fractions to summarize data
- obtain simple summary statistics, for example, mean, median, mode
- describe trends in line graphs
- make judgments about the suitability of data representations

MATERIALS

- calculators
- materials to make graphs

Good Questions and Teacher Notes

1. What might this be the graph of?

Are children's suggestions reasonable? Discuss why some suggestions are more plausible than others.

2. The average of three numbers is 7.1. One of the numbers is 11.2. What might the other numbers be?

Note the methods children use to do this. Let them use calculators if they wish. Can they give a range of responses?

3. There are five people in a family and their average age is 20. What might their ages be?

> It might be helpful to discuss what a family is (many definitions are acceptable). One method to solve the question is to use the total of 100. The other is to balance the ages above and below 20.

4. A basketball player calculated her statistics on her own goal shooting. Over 11 games, her mean (average) score was 6, the median was 7, and the mode was 8. What might her scores be in each of the games?

> The total of the scores is 66. One possible answer is 1, 2, 3, 4, 5, 7, 7, 8, 8, 8, 13. Note if children understand each of the terms.

5. The mean is 5. The median is 6. There are eight scores. What might the scores be?

> Note that, since there are eight scores, for 6 to be the median then the fourth score and the fifth score must be 6, or else they must be evenly spaced around 6, such as 5 and 7. Can the children list all of the possible scores?

6. This is the result of a survey of children in fifth grade at a school similar to this one. Show the data in some different ways.

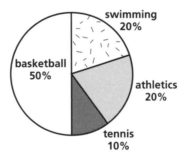

> Note how children approach this. Do they decide how many children are in the class first? Do they realize that there must be an even number of children in the class? Allow time to share their presentations of alternative ways to present the data and discuss which are the most effective.

Good Questions for Math Teaching

7. We did a survey of a class. These are the results.

How many children are in the class? Represent the data in a different way.

Ask children to justify their figure for the number of children in the class. Do they realize that their representations will depend on whatever scale they choose to use? Are they aware that each symbol might represent more than one animal?

8. This is the number of children talking in the class over a period of 30 minutes. What time of day might it be?

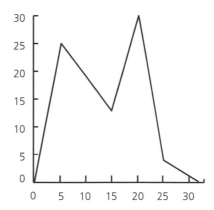

Before starting, discuss with the class how they interpret the graph. After working on the task, ask children to justify their responses. Can they give more than one response?

Chance and Data